*This would be a vital mess[...]
particularly in this current mome[...]
gentleness of Christ seems so [...]
production-line of Christendom. But I am commending
here not just the value of this message but also the
values of its messenger. Paul Friend is one of the most
thoughtful and fiercely humble leaders I know. He has
sown his life faithfully over many years into the young
people of the South West of England, consistently
tending his own soul whilst attending to his own personal
relationships—not least with Jesus himself.*
**Pete Greig, 24-7 Prayer International
and Emmaus Rd UK**

*Growing in true humility is hard but every aspiring leader
needs more of it. This book is a gift to us all. Paul's life
and leadership is mostly characterised by humility, so I
can't think of a better person to be capturing this much
needed insight and wisdom.*
**Pete Wynter, Director of Leadership College London
and Vicar of St Paul's Hammersmith**

*A timely book that will challenge, inspire and offer
practical help for any who seek to follow Christ and lead
with humility. Written with down-to-earth honesty by a
gifted leader who seeks, with humility,
to live what he teaches.*
**Revd Roy Searle, Co-founder of the Northumbria
Community, Past President and Pioneer Ambassador of
the Baptist Union of Great Britain and leadership
mentor, spiritual director and writer.**

Now more than ever we need to rediscover humility in leadership. And we need to do so with fierce commitment. And Paul is ideally placed to write such a book. Over many years he has not only proved his own fierce humility (which he would obviously deny) but it is also evident in the organisation he has led and shaped. Instead of me writing this, it should be any one of the SWYM staff team or students, who can testify more than anyone to what the contents of this book looks like in real life. The church and society today need leaders who read this book and put it into practice. Thank you, Paul, for writing it and demonstrating it.
The Rt Rev James Grier, Bishop of Plymouth

Recovering the protective power of humility in our leadership feels like the most pressing call for the church in the West right now. It's the antidote to the toxic cultures and aggressive models of leadership in churches, charities, organisations and movements that harm, rather than heal hearts. Paul has a gentle way of speaking fiercely about the beauty and power of humble leadership. To my mind, he's earned the right to do so. Avoiding self-righteous smugness as well as despair, Paul guides his readers through a journey of what it might look like to live and lead like Jesus; with courage, grace and above all, humility.
Rachel Gardner is Youth Innovation Lead at St Lukes Blackburn and Director National Partnerships at Youthscape

A timely and prophetic message that counters the popular trend within the world and the Church. The book's biblical wisdom had me repeatedly saying, 'Amen!' Truly a word that is in season.
Steve Uppal, Senior Leader All Nations

No one I know embodies fierce humility with as much joy and consistency as Paul Friend. He leads with excellence and kindness. He has captured some of his life stories and learnings in this brilliant, helpful book. His writing is wise, honest and practical—much like his life!
Canon Sarah Yardley, Mission Lead, Creation Fest UK

A profoundly timely, practical and challenging call to return to the kind of humble leadership needed for the age we find ourselves in.
Gavin Calver, CEO Evangelical Alliance

FIERCE
HUMILITY

Leading teams in the way of Jesus

Copyright © 2023 Paul Friend

The moral right of the author has been asserted.

Apart from any fair dealing for the purposes of research or private study, or criticism or review, as permitted under Copyright, Design and Patents Act 1998, this publication may only be reproduced, stored or transmitted, in any form or by any means, with prior permission in writing of the publishers, or in any case of the reprographic reproduction in accordance with the terms of licences issued by the Copyright Licensing Agency. Enquiries concerning reproduction outside these terms should be sent to the publishers.

PublishU Ltd

www.PublishU.com

Scripture taken from the Holy Bible, New King James Version,
© 1982 by Thomas Nelson, Inc.
All rights reserved.

Scripture from the Holy Bible, New International Version®, NIV®.
Copyright © 1973, 1978, 1984, 2011 by Biblica, Inc.™ Used by permission of Zondervan. All rights reserved worldwide.

Scripture taken from the Holy Bible, New Living Translation,
copyright ©1996, 2004, 2007
by Tyndale House Foundation. Used by permission of Tyndale House Publishers, Inc.,
Carol Stream, IL 60188. All rights reserved.

All rights of this publication are reserved.

Thanks

There are so many people I'd like to thank for enabling this book to become a reality.

As always, it was a team effort. I'd like to firstly thank my family: Jo, my wife, for always loving, supporting and encouraging me to keep going; and for my boys Zach and Charlie, for their patient support and keeping me humble with their cheeky comments. I'd like to thank my wider family, especially my parents for their constant support and interest in all I'm doing and for their love and care.

I'd like to say a huge thank you to SWYM (South West Youth Ministries) for giving me the opportunity to take a sabbatical and supporting me in the writing of this book. The trustees released me for those twelve weeks in early 2023, for which I'm very grateful, but I'd also like to thank them all for their trust, encouragement, accountability and support over the last eighteen years that we've worked so closely together.

I'd also like to thank the Board for their support financially to help make this book happen. The staff of SWYM are a huge delight to lead; I'm so grateful for all the staff both now and over the years who have allowed me to learn, make mistakes and try and work out what it means to lead well together. Finally, to the trainees down the years, thank you for the privilege of working with you all. Being a part of shaping and developing SWYM has been such a privilege and one for which I'm very grateful.

I'd also like to thank those who encouraged me to write this book, especially Pete Gilbert who mentored me for many years and who has written this foreword for me. I'd also like to thank Henry and Jenny for their support and for enabling this book to become a reality.

Finally, I'd like to thank so many friends for their support and encouragement and lots of laughs and banter which all help me to not take myself too seriously and to do all I can to pursue humility.

Contents

Foreword

Introduction

Chapter 1 Fierce Humility - a Call to Arms

Humbling Ourselves Before God

Chapter 2 Fiercely for the Praise/Recognition of the Father Not the Crowd

Chapter 3 Fiercely Relying on the Father Not Own Strength or Gifting

Chapter 4 Fiercely Seeking Time Alone With the Father

Chapter 5 Fiercely Resting

Humbling Ourselves Before Others

Chapter 6 Fiercely Releasing Not Controlling

Chapter 7 Fiercely Vulnerable and Accountable

Chapter 8 Fiercely Forgiving

Chapter 9 Fiercely United

Chapter 10 Fiercely Serving

Concluding Thoughts

PAUL FRIEND

Foreword
By Pete Gilbert

Anyone for an oxymoron? You might think that someone audacious enough to think they could write a book about humility has created just that: an oxymoron. And, indeed, that the words 'fierce' and 'humility' can't really go together. But in this book Paul Friend has demonstrated his audacity, his willingness to take surprisingly bold risks and he has made an excellent and biblical connection between ferocious determination and essential humility.

Paul hasn't written this book from some lofty pulpit, six feet above contradiction, as though sorted and sussed in the vital necessity of humble leadership. Because he isn't. Believe me, I've known Paul very well for more than sixteen years, having had the privilege and pleasure of serving him as his mentor for that time. He isn't sussed and sorted!

What he is, however, is ferociously and ruthlessly determined to follow Jesus in His example of servant leadership: of kindness; of gentle firmness, pushing into the Heart of God and ushering others with him. This book is disarmingly honest, real and vulnerable, as Paul outlines his mistakes, his sins (the two are different) and his lessons learned.

Chapter by chapter, we can journey with Paul as he explores one of God's absolutes: the humble God who is the Servant King. From this **absolute**, Paul unpicks and unpacks the value that is humility; of serving, of leadership by example. This **value** can come to shape our

vision for a better way to lead, to learn, to love, to be and do team.

And what I like and think you'll appreciate as much as anything, is that in this book, Paul goes on from **Absolute** to **Value** to **Vision**, to then outline **Goals** and heart-searching soul exercises to help him and us land and live this thing called 'Ferocious Humility'. This book is challengingly practical but 'do-able'.

If ever we needed a time to see lived out truth, to experience authentic integrity, to encounter vulnerable transparency in team and in leadership by humble example, this is that time. Adrift politically, educationally and institutionally in religion, ferocious humility in following Jesus can help us through the morass of hypocrisy, false news, corruption and the self-serving, self-aggrandising abuse of power and of people which we all too often collide with in the world and, sadly, in the church around us.

I can testify that this book speaks of Paul's actual experience: the highs and, more importantly, the lows. With a teachable heart, Paul has sought the path of ferocious humility and aspires to pursue it and Jesus still further. My hope and prayer for myself and for you as you read and apply the gems contained here, is that we will do likewise.

Read on...

FIERCE HUMILITY

PAUL FRIEND

Introduction

One of my most humbling moments as a leader was when I was asked to speak for the first time as a member of staff for South West Youth Ministries (SWYM). I had been given the topic 'accountability and vulnerability', so I spent time preparing and nervously came to speak thinking to myself, "I really need to do a good job here."

My keenness to prove that I was worthy of my new role was definitely present at the back of my mind, but I was trying to focus on the job at hand. I had felt led to focus on David and Jonathan's relationship in the Old Testament—a close, brotherly relationship characterised by accountability. What could possibly go wrong?

I got up and things seemed to be going well. As I got to the climax of the talk, I explained that when David committed adultery with Bathsheba it was Nathan not Jonathan who rebuked him. I led up to this key moment in the talk where I asked dramatically, "Where was Jonathan? Where was he?"

As I paused for effect someone from the back of the room shouted, "He was dead!" They were, of course, completely correct! I stood there with my face getting redder and redder as I realised that there was no way to fudge my way out of this—I just had to admit my mistake and try to land the talk whilst acknowledging that I looked like an idiot. I was utterly humbled and embarrassed and wanted the ground to swallow me up. Perhaps you can relate to that moment of shame, where you have been exposed and have no way out of it. It is humbling.

This kind of experience, however, is more about being humbled than humbling yourself. It is important to make clear from the outset that there is a big difference between lowering ourselves before God and others (humbling ourselves) and making a fool of yourself (being humbled).

In Matthew 23:11–12, Jesus outlines an instruction and a warning, "The greatest among you shall be your servant. For those who exalt themselves will be humbled and those who humble themselves will be exalted[1]." It's vital we pay close attention to Jesus' words here: 'those who humble themselves.'

This shows that humbling ourselves is what we are seeking to achieve. Furthermore, Jesus shows us that we are responsible for humbling ourselves—humility is not something gifted to us but an attitude and posture we must choose to intentionally engage ourselves in.

Over the last few years, the character of political leaders both here and across the globe has been found severely lacking. The constant stories of abuse of power, inappropriate behaviour, lying, control and pursuit of personal gain are exhaustingly depressing. Sadly, the church has not been set apart in this area either. Heart-wrenching stories of exactly the same issues abound and I don't know about you, but I've had enough.

What is it going to take to change the picture? I wonder, have we built structures and stages that have fed prideful leadership even in our churches? The rise of social media

---

[1] Holy Bible, Matthew 23:11–12, New International Version®, NIV® Copyright ©1973, 1978, 1984, 2011 by Biblica

and the Covid pandemic lockdowns led to lots of churches developing more visual advertising and services streamed on every platform. The challenge for leaders was to not give in to comparison when comparison was all around and to not view success based upon reach and viewing figures. How do we lead humbly when we feel the pressure to hype and sell what we have to offer? How do we fight for humility in our teams when there is a competitiveness that bubbles up within our hearts?

And yet amid all these questions and challenges, I'm drawn back to the person and work of Jesus: the image of the invisible God. The One often described and painted as the meek and mild Jesus—the humble servant. He is both the incarnate Son and King of Kings and yet described himself as gentle and humble in heart.

We all know that humility is a quality to be admired, even sought after, such that the world of business has adopted the model of servant leadership. Yet the word 'humble' is often still understood as weak, a pushover or lacking in real directional leadership. Christoph Secklet, from the ESCP Business School, confirms this saying that, "Unfortunately, in today's daily language, humility is often associated with negative aspects such as low self-esteem or inferior sense of worth."[2] Robert Greenleaf adds, "Servant leaders differ from other persons of goodwill because they act on what they believe... To the worldly, servant-leaders may seem naïve."[3]

---

[2] Christoph Secklet, https://www.weforum.org/agenda/2021/09/humility-important-world-of-work/

[3] Robert Greenleaf, Who is the Servant Leader, International Journal on Servant Leadership, Spokane, 2007, Pg 27-28

Jesus' personal character was what shaped his leadership and influence. When I look at how he led his team, the lack of fortune, pursuit of comfort, the regular retreat from the crowds and consistent releasing of others makes me stop and wonder how we, as the church in the West, have got it so wrong. David Guzik agrees saying. "It is unfortunate that many of the followers of Jesus imitate the leadership philosophy and style of the scribes and Pharisees more than the style of Jesus."[4] Andrew Murray, author of the classic 'Humility—The Beauty of Holiness'[5], writes, "The call to humility has been largely ignored in the church, because its true nature and importance has not been understood."[6]

It is concerning to me that something so core to the person and the work of Jesus has been overlooked in our discipleship and in our leadership. Surely, as Murray says, "Meekness and lowliness of heart are supposed to be the distinguishing features of the disciple as they were of the Master."[7]

For the Christian, Jesus is our teacher and our example—the one we are called to follow and to imitate. We are to walk in the dust of our Rabbi, to follow him everywhere

---

[4] David Guzik, Enduring Word, Matthew 23, 2018

[5] Andrew Murray, Humility – The Beauty of Holiness, Aneko Press, Revised Edition, 2016

[6] Andrew Murray, Humility – The Beauty of Holiness, Aneko Press, Revised Edition, 2016, Pg 3-4

[7] Andrew Murray, Humility – The Beauty of Holiness, Aneko Press, Revised Edition, 2016, Pg 4

and become like Him. Throughout his life and ministry, Jesus modelled in his actions and spoke frequently of the importance of humility. It wasn't just a nice sermon on the topic but his whole life screamed "humility": from the incarnation to his death on the cross and even his cooking of breakfast after his resurrection. Time and again, as I have come back to the humility of Jesus, I have noticed within Jesus' life and ministry a ferocity in his humility. This is not a gentle, quiet humility, quite the opposite; this is a humility that fights against pride in both himself and his followers. A humility that confronts the arrogant and proud religious leaders, fierceness that says, "get behind me Satan"[8] to the very disciple he had just promised to build his church upon. It's a fierce humility that confronts, fights for and refuses to allow any room in its kingdom for pride, hypocrisy, arrogance or self-promotion.

If we are all honest, we don't really like talking about pride and humility, it's a little too close to the bone for us. We know we all struggle with thoughts and heart attitudes of pride and to humble ourselves can be painful, embarrassing and costly. However, it is the life to which we have been called and, therefore, one which we must embrace; and one, I believe, that we must fiercely pursue. To seek fierce humility and the irradiation of pride in our lives, our teams and our ministry is a lifelong mission that must be at the forefront of our thinking, speaking and actions if we are to make any progress towards our aim at all.

---

[8] Holy Bible, Matthew 16:23, New International Version®, NIV® Copyright ©1973, 1978, 1984, 2011 by Biblica

It is important to say from the outset that I am not writing this book from the position of believing that I am fiercely humble myself, far from it! The motivation comes from what I believe is a deep, Christ-implanted desire in my heart to pursue humility. I have a long list of examples where my heart, my mind, my voice and actions have been far from humble. In truth, it is a daily battle for me to place myself before the God who sees me. I am writing not out of success but out of failure; not out of accomplishment but out of a hunger to walk more like Jesus and recognising my utter need of Him to transform me.

I guess, if you started a book on humility and the author said anything other than what I've just written you'd probably shut the book right now, but it is the honest truth.

I am writing not because I have a lot to say, but because I have a lot to learn and I'd love you to go on the journey with me of dying to pride, re-imagining our leadership and walking in humility in a ferocious way that fights for humility in our own hearts but also in those we lead and walk alongside.

This book is for you if you share a desire for humility, if you come with a hunger for change and a teachable spirit that cries, "He must become greater, I must become less."[9] It does not matter whether you lead a church, business or charity; a team in church or the workplace; a worship team, catering team, PA and visuals team or lead within your family or in a home group or missional

---

[9] Holy Bible, John 3:30, New International Version®, NIV® Copyright ©1973, 1978, 1984, 2011 by Biblica

community. Whatever your leadership setting or your place of influence, I believe the principles and practices we explore over the coming pages will hopefully inspire, challenge and call you on to a deeper place with lower levels of self that enable you to lead more in the way of Jesus rather than in the way of this world. I hope you enjoy the journey but if you do maybe don't tell me! I don't want to get proud!

It is my conviction that the Church in the West has moved and drifted so far from Jesus' model of ministry and leadership that we need to get back to His basics.

Chapter 1
Fierce Humility - A Call to Arms

"At every stage of our Christian development and in every sphere of our Christian discipleship, pride is the greatest enemy and humility our greatest friend."
John Stott[10]

"When I survey the wondrous cross, on which the Prince of Glory died, My richest gain I count but loss and pour contempt on all my pride."
Isaac Watts[11]

A few years ago, a similar ministry to ours at SWYM popped up right on our doorstep. We had spent eighteen years at this point building a regional training and placement model for youth and children's workers, working with churches across a number of different denominations and felt like things were going well. And then something very similar sprung up as the 'new thing' right next to us. We weren't initially excited, rather a bit put out.

---

[10] John Stott, Pride, Humility, and God," in *Alive to God*, eds. JI Packer & Loren Wilkinson, (Downers Grove, IL: InterVarsity Press, 1992), Pg 119

[11] Isaac Watts, When I survey the Wondrous Cross, Hymns and Spiritual Songs, 1707

A few days after the announcement, I received a call from a local leader who started to tell me that what we offered was better. Their kind-hearted intention to encourage me unintentionally served to stroke my ego. My response was that I was choosing to pray for this new ministry every day—choosing to pray that God might bless what they were doing, increase and grow their influence and reach and that they would go further than we ever had. The person on the end of the phone stopped me and said, "Oh Paul you, are so holy." Immediately, I stopped them and replied, "I'm really not. The reason I am praying this prayer every day is that I have to; if I don't, competitiveness, fear and anxiety grows in my heart that causes me to give in to pride. I will keep praying this every day until I really mean it."

The conversation quickly moved on, but I remember it because it was a moment of honestly sharing what was going on in my heart in response to threat. Internally, I was fighting a fierce battle every day to stop my selfish defensiveness from overflowing into pride, competitiveness and fear.

Walking in humility and fighting against pride is a complicated and challenging journey. But before we explore something of Jesus' example and how we might walk in humility and fight for humility in our teams, we need to first define what pride is and then, secondly, what humility is. Finally, we will look at what I'm arguing fierce humility really is.

What is pride?

You might wonder why I'm choosing to talk about pride first rather than humility. If humility is the goal, then why are we starting with the enemy? Since humility is part of the character of God, why are we not starting there? The simple answer is that to fully understand humility we must grasp the full extent of what pride is and how it seeks to make war on our character. From an understanding of our enemy, we can begin to walk towards humility.

I wonder how you might define pride. What would you say it was in essence? What are the consequences of pride? And what are the warning signs that it is shaping your words and actions?

A dictionary definition defines pride as "feeling of deep pleasure or satisfaction derived from one's own achievements, the achievements of those with whom one is closely associated, or from qualities or possessions that are widely admired."[12]

Linked to the word pride there are the words "arrogant" and "arrogance" which can be defined as "having or revealing an exaggerated sense of one's own importance or abilities". Here we begin to get a picture of how pride is all about self—about our achievements, qualities, possessions or sense of importance.

Pride is what I saw in my toddler who refused to apologise, even though he knew he was in the wrong and, therefore, stayed for an extra minute on the naughty

---

[12] Collins English Dictionary. Copyright © HarperCollins Publishers, Ninth edition (4 Jun. 2007)

step. Pride is what I see in me when my first thought when hearing of another's success is not immediate joy but rather jealousy.

Biblically, we might expect to start at the beginning of Genesis to find the origin of pride at the fall. It is important to recognise that pride had already been on the scene for some time before Eve tucked into the apple. Key passages in Ezekiel and Isaiah tell of the fall of Satan and we are told that it was pride that was at the root of his rebellion.

In Ezekiel 28:17 God declares, "Your heart was proud because of your beauty; you corrupted your wisdom for the sake of your splendour.[13] And then in Isaiah 14:12–17: "You said in your heart, 'I will ascend to heaven; above the stars of God I will set my throne on high; I will sit on the mount of assembly in the far reaches of the north; I will ascend above the heights of the clouds; I will make myself like the Most High.'"[14]

These verses show how Satan's fall was a selfish endeavour led by a desire to be like God. Satan wanted to set himself up as a god: he desired splendour,to be lifted up, 'ascended,' 'my throne on high'. RT Kendall defines pride as 'When sinful human beings aspire to the status and position of God and refuse to acknowledge

---

[13] Holy Bible, Ezekiel 28:17, New International Version®, NIV® Copyright ©1973, 1978, 1984, 2011 by Biblica

[14] Holy Bible, Isaiah 14:12–17, New International Version®, NIV® Copyright ©1973, 1978, 1984, 2011 by Biblica

their dependence on Him.'[15] This definition seems to mirror what we see in that first act of pride by Satan. Charles Bridges also states: "Pride lifts up one's heart against God and contends for supremacy with Him."[16]

The fall of Satan described in Isaiah highlights a couple of key things about pride. Firstly, 'He said in his heart.' It started with a thought that led to a plan being birthed in his heart. He said in his heart that he wanted glory, praise and honour. Notice, he didn't say he wants to be above God but like the Most High, to be above other angelic beings, to be exalted above others.

Secondly, he used the phrase "I will..." The thought spoken in his heart led to a determination to act, to take matters into his own hands. Pride takes root in the heavenly realms and as Jesus later states in Luke 10:18, "I saw Satan fall like lighting from heaven."[17] Here, we see how pride from the very beginning led to a fall.

The Message paraphrase gives a fresh perspective on this familiar proverb from Proverbs 16:18, "First pride, then the crash—the bigger the ego, the harder the fall."[18]

---

[15] C.J.Mahoney, Humility - True Greatness, Soverign Grace Ministries, 2005, Pg 31

[16] Charles Bridges, Commentary on Proverbs (Geneva), 1968

[17] Holy Bible, Luke 10:18, New International Version®, NIV® Copyright ©1973, 1978, 1984, 2011 by Biblica

[18] Holy Bible, Proverbs 16 :18, New International Version®, NIV® Copyright ©1973, 1978, 1984, 2011 by Biblica

Derek Prince, in his book 'Pride verses Humility' reflects on the fall of Satan saying, "The Scriptures reveal clearly that both he and all the angels who followed him were driven out from the presence of God due to their rebellion. Notice that the root of rebellion was pride. It was Lucifer's beauty and wisdom that caused his pride. His pride then caused his rebellion. The result when he exalted himself was that he was cast down."[19]

Once again, we see here that it was Satan's heart where pride was conceived and then came the determination to act giving birth to rebellion.

Pride and the battle for supremacy with God was firmly established before Adam and Eve arrive on the scene in Genesis 2 and then succumb to pride in Genesis 3. The serpent tempts Eve and even as he tempts, he says in verse five that, "God knows that when you eat from it your eyes will be opened and you will be like God".[20]

The same issue of seeking equality with God appears here. Eve is tempted and sees 'that the fruit of the tree was good for food and pleasing to the eye, also desirable for gaining wisdom, she took some and ate it. She also gave some to her husband, who was with her and he ate it'.[21] Notice here how she is tempted by pride in gaining wisdom to be better than others. Derek Prince adds,

---

[19] Derek Prince, Pride versus Humility, Derek Prince Ministries, 2016, Pg 31

[20] Holy Bible, Genesis 3:5, New International Version®, NIV® Copyright ©1973, 1978, 1984, 2011 by Biblica

[21] Holy Bible, Genesis 3:6, New International Version®, NIV® Copyright ©1973, 1978, 1984, 2011 by Biblica

"Pride is seeking to be independent of God...They simply made a personal decision that they could do without Him, that they did not need Him."[22] Pride says, "I am enough. I know best. I am right, you are wrong. I am the most important. I...I...I..." Pride worships the trinity of me, myself and I.

It is so easy to look at Satan's fall and the fall of humanity and point the finger at Satan and Adam and Eve, but the truth is the same pride is at war with our own souls. Mahoney writes, "The real issue here is not if pride exists in your heart, it's where pride exists and how pride is being expressed in your life." [23]

Pride is an issue we all face and pride sets us up against God, fights to be exalted above others and ultimately seeks independence from and rebellion against our Creator. Jennifer Cole Wright describes the danger of pride when she says in her book 'The Moral Psychology of Humility' that, "We each stand, phenomenologically speaking, at the centre of the universe. This inherent centredness biases our experience of our own needs, desires, interests, beliefs, goals and values as being more immediate and urgent than those others."[24]

---

[22] Derek Prince, Pride versus Humility, Derek Prince Ministries, 2016, Pg 74

[23] C.J.Mahoney, Humility - True Greatness, Soverign Grace Ministries, 2005, Pg 29

[24] Jennifer Cole Wright, The Moral Psychology of Humility, Routledge, 2020, Pg 10

In the New Testament James 4:6 says, "God opposes the proud but shows grace to the humble."[25] This verse is beautifully blunt as we see the forcefulness of God's attitude to pride. He opposes the proud. He comes against it. When I read the word 'opposes' it makes me think of a rugby scrum. That moment when one team uses all their strength and force together to push against or to overpower the opposition. This is a harsh warning and challenges me as I really don't want God to be opposing me. I don't want to be setting myself up against him by allowing pride to take root in my heart. By contrast, the promise for those who are humble is that God will show grace—He will be gracious and kind. He will be 'for' those who humble themselves.

RT Kendall continues by saying that, "Pride is the lack of the fear of God."[26] It's where we have a wrong view of God; one that gives us room to promote ourselves alongside Him in our heart. Ultimately, Kendall says that "Pride is the root of the need to prove ourselves."[27] Pride is bred from a place of insecurity.

In his book 'Mere Christianity', CS Lewis re-enforces this viewpoint: "As long as you are proud you cannot know God. A proud man is always looking down on things and people: and, of course, as long as you are looking down

---

[25] Holy Bible, James 4:6, New International Version®, NIV® Copyright ©1973, 1978, 1984, 2011 by Biblica

[26] R.T.Kendall, The Power of Humility, Charisma House, 2011, Pg xiv

[27] R.T.Kendall, The Power of Humility, Charisma House, 2011, Pg 36

you cannot see something that is above you."[28] Pride has an ability to disable us from drawing close to God and, ultimately, we can see in the example of the fall of Satan and humanity that pride is at the root of sin. In fact, you could argue that pride is at the root of all sin. Perhaps that is why Jesus fought so fiercely against it: he knew it was the root issue, the number one problem, the epidemic in humanity. He knew that pride must be called out, done away with and something different taking its place and that something different was humility.

What is humility?

Rick Warren famously said, "True humility is not thinking less of yourself; it is thinking of yourself less."[29] This is a helpful way of thinking about humility as it is a move away from self-obsession to living an others-focused life. But is this all humility is? Andrew Murray takes it further saying that "Humility is the disappearance of self in the vision and understanding that God is all."[30]

Here we have an expanded view that humility is developed when we have an understanding that God is all, that He is enough for us. That He can be trusted with our lives and that He is King.

---

[28] C.S.Lewis, Mere Christianity, Harper Collins, 1952, Pg 124

[29] Rick Warren, The Purpose Driven Life, Zondervan, 2002, Pg 148

[30] Andrew Murray, Humility – The Beauty of Holiness, Aneko Press, Revised Edition, 2016, Pg 42

CJ Mahoney defines humility saying that, "Humility is honestly accessing ourselves in light of God's holiness and our sinfulness."[31] There is a link, then, between how we view ourselves and how we view God that shapes humility in us. Andrew Murray continues this thought, adding that humility "is not a thing which we bring to God, or He gives. Humility is simply the sense of entire nothingness, which comes when we see how truly God is all and in which we make way for God to be all". [32]

There is something about coming to the end of ourselves and recognising our need for and reliance upon God that creates humility. Abraham Lincoln, when reflecting on his leadership, said, "I have been driven many times upon my knees by the overwhelming conviction that I had nowhere else to go. My own wisdom and that of all about me seemed insufficient for that day."[33]

This is further backed up by Blanchard, Hodges and Hendry in 'Lead like Jesus Revisited': "Humility is a heart attitude that reflects a keen understanding of your limitations and even inability to accomplish something on your own."[34] Humility is about a complete dependency on

---

[31] C.J.Mahoney, Humility - True Greatness, Soverign Grace Ministries, 2005, Pg 22

[32] Andrew Murray, Humility-The Beauty of Holiness, Aneko Press, Revised Edition, 2016, Pg 4

[33] Abraham Lincoln, https://www.thoughtco.com/abraham-lincoln-quotations-everyone-should-know-1773576

[34] Blanchard, Hodges and Hendry, Lead like Jesus Revisited; W Publishing, 2016

God—humility comes as we pray the words of John the Baptist found in John 3:30, "He must become greater, I must become less."[35]

In Isaiah 66:2, God describes those He is looking for: "This is the one to whom I will look: he who is humble and contrite in spirit and trembles at my word."[36] The Father desires those who will humble themselves. Andrew Murray says, "Humility draws the gaze of our Sovereign God" [37] whereas in comparison Psalm 5 says, "The arrogant cannot stand in your presence."[38] This is critical: is it not motivation enough that God wants us to be humble and that if we are arrogant, we cannot stand in His presence? This isn't a command to seek humility before a powerful, proud God. Humility is part of who He is—His character. For He is not proud or arrogant but humble. In fact, Jesus described himself as "gentle and humble in heart".[39]

---

[35] Holy Bible, John 3:30, New International Version®, NIV® Copyright ©1973, 1978, 1984, 2011 by Biblica

[36] Holy Bible, Isaiah 66:2, New International Version®, NIV® Copyright ©1973, 1978, 1984, 2011 by Biblica

[37] C.J.Mahoney, Humility - True Greatness, Soverign Grace Ministries, 2005, Pg 19

[38] Holy Bible, Psalm 5:5, New International Version®, NIV® Copyright ©1973, 1978, 1984, 2011 by Biblica

[39] Holy Bible, Matthew 11:29, New International Version®, NIV® Copyright ©1973, 1978, 1984, 2011 by Biblica

As the image of the invisible God, Jesus became literal flesh and by doing so modelled humility for the world to see. One of my favourite passages in Scripture is found in Philippians 2, where Paul encourages us all to "in humility value others above ourselves"[40] and that, "in your relationships with one another, have the same mindset as Christ Jesus".[41]

Here, Paul is saying that Jesus is our absolute example; we are to follow Him in how he modelled humility for us. The Greek word for mindset or attitude in our English translations is "phroneo" which put simply means "our thinking, our feelings, emotions and our actions". Perhaps this is where the bracelets asking, 'What Would Jesus Do?' originated. When it comes to humility, think like Jesus, act like Jesus, feel like Jesus. This historic hymn of praise explains so well why we should base it all on him:

He made himself nothing,

taking the very nature of a servant,

being made in human likeness.[42]

Despite being part of the Godhead with everything at his disposal, he chooses to humble himself: The Son of God, the timeless one entering our time, the omnipresent one

---

[40] Holy Bible, Philippians 2:3, New International Version®, NIV® Copyright ©1973, 1978, 1984, 2011 by Biblica

[41] Holy Bible, Philippians 2:5, New International Version®, NIV® Copyright ©1973, 1978, 1984, 2011 by Biblica

[42] Holy Bible, Philippians 2:7, New International Version®, NIV® Copyright ©1973, 1978, 1984, 2011 by Biblica

restricted to a baby's body, the all-powerful one choosing to make himself dependant on a teenage mum in a highly dangerous situation. The King of Kings humbles himself, not born in a palace to the rich and important but born into obscurity and soon to be a refugee; welcomed by society's leasts, the shepherds. He humbled himself more than we will ever understand or comprehend as he became human. When summarising the phrase, "He made himself nothing," RT Kendall explains that the "literal translation means that the God-man emptied Himself of glory."[43] He emptied himself of all he had. Jesus didn't stop there although this act of humility was significant enough, but he goes further still:

And being found in appearance as a man,

He humbled himself,

By becoming obedient to death

Even death on a cross[44]

He humbles himself again. His coming was an act, a display of humility, His death the ultimate expression of the humility of the King of Kings. He humbled himself and was obedient to death and the worst death humanity has ever conceived. Jesus' arrival was humble, his death humble, his life and teaching (which we will explore more) a demonstration of a life of humility. He is our example. He is our inspiration for, as Andrew Murray, said, "Let us

---

[43] R.T.Kendall, The Power of Humility, Charisma House, 2011, Pg 60

[44] Holy Bible, Philippians 2:8, New International Version®, NIV® Copyright ©1973, 1978, 1984, 2011 by Biblica

study the character of Christ until our souls are filled with the love and admiration of his lowliness."[45] The classic Sunday school answer, which was always the answer to every question, is true again. The secret to humility is simply Jesus. It's why John Owen said, "Fill your affections with the cross of Christ."[46] It's why RT Kendell wrote, "Regarding trying to be humble. Do not try so hard; just look to Jesus."[47]

His life and death embodied and fleshed out God's character—His other-worldly, other-kingdom way of being. The upside-down kingdom would not be defined by power, prestige or fighting to the top. A way not forged in self-promotion and pride, but one of sacrifice and service, one so very different from all we'd ever seen or known.

But the problem is that we might be attracted to this different way, but the old system, the old way of thinking, feeling, behaving has already captured our hearts. As CJ Mahoney put it, "We cannot free ourselves from pride and selfish ambition; a divine rescue is absolutely necessary."[48]

---

[45] Andrew Murray, Humility - The Beauty of Holiness, Aneko Press, Revised Edition, 2016, Pg 5

[46] John Owen, On the nature, power, deceit, and prevalence of indwelling sin in believers, For Chalmers and Collins, 1825, Pg 199

[47] R.T Kendall, The Power of Humility, Charisma House, 2011, Pg 173

[48] C.J.Mahoney, Humility - True Greatness, Sovereign Grace Ministries, 2005, Pg 52

We cannot conquer pride. Prince, reflecting on God's response to pride wrote, "You see, God's answer to pride is always humility. The more God encountered pride, the more He displayed humility."[49] Jesus holds the key to humility. Out of a humble heart flows servanthood, forgiveness and grace, a selfless promotion of others and so much more, but it cannot be forced. It cannot be achieved through a try-harder mentality. Jesus is the way as well as the truth and the life. Jesus' way is the way of death and so to follow him, our will, our self, our pride must first die and then God can recreate in us a humble heart.

I love this prayer from CJ Mahaney, "Father, I want to stand as close to the cross as I possibly can, because it's harder for me to be arrogant when I'm there."[50] If we want to be those who walk in humility, this must be our prayer, too. As leaders, we not only care first and foremost about our own hearts but also of those we are leading. We want to walk humbly before our God, but we also want to create teams and cultures that model humility and fight for it fiercely in our setting.

What is fierce humility?

The humility of Jesus is often portrayed and described as the meek and mild Jesus. I have seen so many paintings of Jesus gazing longingly into the distance, a calm and serene figure. As stated above, Jesus is our role model

---

[49] Derek Prince, Pride versus Humility, Derek Prince Ministries, 2016, Pg 60

[50] C.J.Mahoney, Humility - True Greatness, Sovereign Grace Ministries, 2005, Pg 68

and the best example of humility. However, when it comes to the issue of pride in either his disciples or in the Pharisees or political leaders, he is far from quiet, serene and retiring. Jesus waged war on pride; he was outspoken, blunt to the point of rude and spoke harshly to confront people with the reality of what was going on in their hearts, whether they were ready to receive it or not. Jesus was not the warrior king the Jews wanted who would overthrow the Romans. Jesus had a more important superpower to overthrow — one that would outlast the Roman Empire: the power of pride and the sin that is birthed from it. Jesus may not have taken up physical weapons, instructing Peter to lay down his sword at his arrest, but Jesus fiercely fought in his words and actions to do away with sin, death, Satan and pride as the root of it all.

Another leader who talked about the need for fierce leadership was Winston Churchill. He said, "Do not be fobbed off with mere personal success or acceptance. You will make all kinds of mistakes; but as long as you are generous and true and also fierce, you cannot hurt the world or even seriously distress her." [51] Whatever you think of the message, there is some wisdom in those words: we will make mistakes but a fierceness and a determination in living generously and in truth is a good way to live.

We're often told that we have to fight our way to the top in this world, but if we want to follow in the way of Jesus, we have to fight our way to the bottom. We have to learn what it is to lower ourselves. It is a bit like rescuers

---

[51] Winston Churchill, https://richardlangworth.com/success

digging their way down through the rubble of a collapsed building to find those buried beneath—digging deeper, going lower, seeking to serve, to rescue others, to never give up until they are found and every stone has been turned. When the buried person is found, the rescuer often disappears into the background as the rescued one shares their story. It is the one who was rescued who shares their story not the rescuer.

The Gospels are littered with records of Jesus' rebukes, teaching and interactions with lots of different types of people. In this book, we will explore some of these encounters to explore how Jesus fought for humility, why perhaps he said what he said and what we can learn so that we too might live a fiercely humble life as we lead in our sphere of influence.

Phrases such as, "Get behind me Satan"; "not so with you"; "he without sin cast the first stone"; "white-washed tombs" and so many more show us that Jesus was not afraid to confront, offend or make a stand for what he knew was so important. Not only did he speak up for humility and against pride, but He also modelled it.

When considering how Jesus modelled humility, we can quickly hold up Jesus' silence under trial or the crucifixion and rightly so. We can also consider washing the disciples' feet; however, we don't so readily reflect on Jesus fleeing from the crowd, moving on from the place of successful ministry and the reality of having nowhere to lay his head. It is my conviction that the Church in the West has moved and drifted so far from Jesus' model of ministry and leadership that we need to get back to His basics.

Church and ministry leadership right now in the 2020s celebrates those on the stage, perceives success in terms of numbers, thinks in terms of strategy of ministry and celebrates the charismatic leader. Perhaps we have got it all wrong. Have we allowed the way the world does leadership to filter into the Church?

In Matthew 20:25-26, "You know that the rulers of the Gentiles lord it over them and their high officials exercise authority over them. Not so with you."[52] Jesus clearly states here that Christian leadership is not the same as leadership in the world. It should be the opposite to ruling over others. Perhaps it's time to fiercely pursue a different type of leadership: a leadership which lowers itself, a leadership which fights for humility in its culture and doesn't allow pride to be left unchecked. What would it look like to lead others with a fierce humility that was more about depth and real relationship than success and status?

Imagine the Church worldwide set apart from the world with leaders who model humility and servant leadership to society. A church so set apart in its 'otherness' that stories of abuse of power, manipulation and competitive in-fighting are silenced. Imagine teams so focused on serving and preferring one another that volunteering or being employed within a ministry setting is described by all as the best vocation in the world. Imagine a Church transformed as the spotless bride ready for her bridegroom.

---

[52] Holy Bible, Matthew 20 v 25-26, New International Version®, NIV® Copyright ©1973, 1978, 1984, 2011 by Biblica

This book is a rallying cry: a call to arms! It is an invitation to live differently, counter-culturally. It's an invitation to personally live lower, to recognise our utter need of God and dependence upon Him—to die to ourselves daily. As we seek this way of Jesus, we then join in the battle to call others to walk the same way: to fiercely confront structures in society, structures in our organisations, our churches, our teams that have been built on self-importance, self-promotion and self-gratification. We wage war on selfish, manipulative, controlling behaviour not as a judge (for there is only one of them and it isn't us) but as a loyal friend.

One of the challenges of fierce humility is this reality: "what we often despise in others is exactly what is so rampant in ourselves."[53] We can be so quick to identify pride in others. Fierce humility, however, is not simply giving ourselves permission to call others out whilst leaving ourselves unchecked. We have to be seeking daily to walk in humility, digging deep into some of the practices we will explore later and then inviting others to come and join us in that same pursuit. Anything other than this is simply judgement, shame and in essence pride disguised as fierce humility.

So right at the start of this book I would ask you, the reader, a question. Will you 'humble yourselves, therefore, under God's mighty hand'[54] and will you pick up your shield and sword to fight? Will you stand for

---

[53] R.T Kendall, The Power of Humility, Charisma House, 2011, Pg 87

[54] Holy Bible, 1 Peter 5 v 6, New International Version®, NIV® Copyright ©1973, 1978, 1984, 2011 by Biblica

humility, fighting fiercely against pride in yourself and those you lead and serve? Will you fiercely set and guard your team culture so that it is marked by humility and grace? Will you fight for a more Christ-like model of leadership—a leadership that is lower, more releasing, more background and more kingdom not empire? This is a call to arms! Will you choose to fight?

As we travel on from here, we will explore a number of inner practices before we look at what living with fierce humility looks like as we engage with our teams. Each chapter revolves around an interaction Jesus had with someone and finishes the chapter with some questions for reflection or discussion. These are designed so that you might use the questions to reflect personally, but you could also use them as a resource with your team about what this might mean for you.

FIERCE HUMILITY

> *Jesus was wholly secure and lived for the praise and recognition of the Father and we are called to do the same.*

Chapter 2
Fiercely for the Praise and Recognition of the Father Not the Crowd

"There is no limit to how far a person can go as long as he doesn't care who gets the credit for it."
A Plaque on President Ronald Reagan's desk

"Everything they do is done for men to see."
Matthew 23:5[55]

When I was ten years old, I got the lead role in our Year Six school production. This could sound more of an achievement than it really was. Growing up in rural Devon, there were only seven children in my school year. I can still remember parts of a song about my character called Sir Spence. I stood centre stage in our little village hall packed full of parents and friends and boldly sang "Sir Spence, Sir Spence, He really is immense!"

I loved being the centre of attention for those few days, something I wasn't that used to as I was not the most popular at primary school. I was at that age: the quiet, shy one, although that changed as I got older and that love of being the centre of attention is one I've had to battle with ever since. Singing and performing there on little stage

---

[55] Holy Bible, Matthew 23 v 5, New International Version®, NIV® Copyright ©1973, 1978, 1984, 2011 by Biblica

blocks and the applause and comments that followed was my first encounter with a need to check my pride. It was a huge confidence-building week for me, which was great, but it was also a week where I had enjoyed the experience a bit too much! After that leading role, I was always looking for opportunities to add sketches into services at church. I was taken under the wing of a local mime enthusiast, leading to several individual performances in churches and even the odd pub over the following three or four years. I took part in several bigger performances that we did at our local Methodist church, including 'Joseph and his Technicolour Dreamcoat' and 'Colby', where I had to dress up as a talking and singing robot of all things!

I will never forget what my mum said to me one Sunday evening as we drove home from church after I had just performed a drama. I was probably a bit too full of myself. She turned from the front passenger seat and said, "Duck and let the glory go to God." That phrase has stuck with me ever since: a very simple but visual image. Duck! In other words, let the praise go past you and let it go to the God who made you and gave you the gifts in the first place.

Receiving praise can be a challenging thing. Some of us can't receive it, brushing it off with a 'no, it wasn't good' or some other dismissive comment, perhaps because we have a poor self-image and can't accept it when others praise us. True humility is not putting ourselves down, this is false humility. Others brush it off to get further affirmation—we need more comments out of a need to be accepted or praised. The word "duck" doesn't mean that we don't acknowledge the hard work, effort and energy we have put into something. A few years ago, a friend challenged me to respond to praise by simply saying, "Thank you." An acknowledgement of the compliment but not fishing for more or asking if they are sure, just simply receiving it. In my experience the "duck" comes later when I'm on my own. Latterly, after big events or moments when thanks or praise have come my way, I try to get out in nature on my own (well, usually with the dog) to thank God for the opportunity. I give praise to Him and ask Him to keep me humble as I find myself alone with Him in the quiet.

I'm not sure if my mum had been reading the work of seventeenth-century Puritan Thomas Watson, but in essence she had modernised his thinking when he wrote, "When we have done anything praiseworthy, we must hide ourselves under the veil of humility and transfer the glory of all we have done to God." [56] The principle of hiding ourselves is a beautiful one: a picture of deliberately counteracting pride by hiding ourselves in God and giving the praise back as a transfer to Him.

Sadly, we have probably all known or experienced leaders who operate out of an attention-seeking, praise and affirmation hunting, driven, defensive and insecure heart and the potential damage, pain and burnout that can follow in their wake. Before we try to explore how we might build healthy cultures as leaders, we must tend to our own hearts first.

---

[56] Thomas Watson, Body of Divinity, The Banner of Truth Trust; New edition, 1983

Jesus as our example in this

Jesus fiercely lived for the recognition of and praise of the Father not for the crowd. At Jesus' baptism, before he has even started his ministry, God the Father speaks over Him saying, "This is my son, with whom I am well pleased." [57]

Some argue this was as much for those around to hear as it was for Jesus, but either way, this encouragement, loving declaration and approval is the basis for all that follows. A similar recognition comes at the transfiguration as again God speaks and says, "This my son, whom I love; with him I am well pleased. Listen to him." [58] Jesus later mentions he can do nothing by himself, he can do only what he sees his Father doing. "For I did not speak on my own, but the Father who sent me commanded me to say all that I have spoken." [59] We get a picture here of the sense of daily obedience and submission Jesus had to the Father.

The Father was the one he was seeking to obey and seeking to be in right standing with. The phrase just before Jesus washed his disciples' feet makes the security and identity of Jesus very clear in John 13:3–4a: "Jesus knew that the Father had put all things under his

---

[57] Holy Bible, Matthew 3:17, New International Version®, NIV® Copyright ©1973, 1978, 1984, 2011 by Biblica

[58] Holy Bible, Matthew 17:5, New International Version®, NIV® Copyright ©1973, 1978, 1984, 2011 by Biblica

[59] Holy Bible, John 12:49–50, New International Version®, NIV® Copyright ©1973, 1978, 1984, 2011 by Biblica

power and that he had come from God and was returning to God; so."[60] I love the word 'so'. As a result of knowing who he was, where he had come from and what God had planned for him, he can get up from the table and wash his disciples' feet. This verse suggests that there was nothing of attention gaining, nothing of selfish endeavour in this act of service but selfless love made possible by knowing who he was.

Jesus' identity and security were found in his relationship with the Father. Does that mean he didn't care about other people? Not at all! He wept with Mary and Martha at the death of Lazarus but his priority, his focus and his decisions were made in the light of what the Father wanted him to do. Kendall wrote, "I reckon the best single word to describe Jesus is His unpretentiousness."[61] It is so true! Jesus didn't need to impress anyone; he was not needing to put himself out there to gain others praise. Our saviour was content with who He was and was focused on what he had been sent to do and fiercely desired the same for his disciples.

In Matthew 23 Jesus confronts both the crowds and his disciples around this topic. It is a challenging passage but one that shows how Jesus not only modelled humility in this area but how he fought for it.

But do not do what they do, for they do not practice what they preach. They tie up heavy, cumbersome loads and put them on other people's shoulders, but they

---

[60] Holy Bible, John 13:3–4a, New International Version®, NIV® Copyright ©1973, 1978, 1984, 2011 by Biblica

[61] R.T Kendall, The Power of Humility, Charisma House, 2011, Pg 56

themselves are not willing to lift a finger to move them. Everything they do is done for people to see. They make their phylacteries wide and the tassels on their garments long, they love the place of honour at banquets and the most important seats in the synagogues: they love to be greeted with respect in the marketplaces and to be called 'Rabbi' by others. [62]

Jesus begins by addressing the burden the Pharisees placed on others which Matthew Henry comments, "They indulged their pride in giving law to others; but consulted their ease in their own practice."[63] Jesus here fiercely confronts hypocrisy. The passage contains a challenge for all leaders, as Anna Case-Winters expertly explains: "As we read these sharp-edged texts today, we are tempted to let them rest in the past as a condemnation of a particular subset of the Pharisees. We locate ourselves among the righteous and know that Jesus is talking not about 'us' but about 'them'. What if, instead, we took the texts as an occasion to examine our own religious life and practice to see if the things Jesus speaks so heatedly against are to be found there? Those who are religious leaders might look particularly closely at what is condemned here. These texts are surely a cautionary tale instructive for religious leaders and all 'would-be' followers of Jesus."[64]

---

[62] Holy Bible, Matthew 23:3–7, New International Version®, NIV® Copyright ©1973, 1978, 1984, 2011 by Biblica

[63] Matthew Henry, Matthew Henry Commentary on the Whole Bible (Complete). Vol. 1. N.p., 1706. http://www.biblestudytools.com/commentaries/matthew-henry-complete

[64] Anna Case Winters, Matthew, Westminster John Knox, 2015

As leaders, we must seek to lead with clean hands and pure hearts and be teachable, quick to repent, slow to judge, quick to show mercy. We must come humbly to these challenging words of Jesus and, like David says in Psalm 139, cry out, "Search me, O God and know my heart: try me and know my thoughts: And see if there be any wicked way in me and lead me in the way everlasting."[65]

Jesus uses a very confrontational phrase: "Everything they do is done for people to see." EVERYTHING – There isn't a thing they do in secret, nothing they do is for God alone to see. No, they lived their lives living for the praise of others. This is the opposite of the way of Jesus. He lived for the praise and recognition of the Father not others whilst the religious leaders did the exact opposite. Jeannine Brown comments on this passage saying that, "They seek honour from people rather than praise from God alone for their religious observance. Nowhere do we hear Jesus faulting their religious practice per se. Instead, he is highly critical of their misplaced focus upon human accolades."[66] Matthew Henry also comments, "But we must not proclaim our good works, with design that others may see them and glorify us." [67] It is so easy for us to find our worth in the praise or affection of others. The

---

[65] Holy Bible, Psalm 139:23–24, New International Version®, NIV® Copyright ©1973, 1978, 1984, 2011 by Biblica

[66] Jeannine Brown & Kyle Roberts, Matthew, Wm. B. Eerdmans Publishing Co, 2018

[67] Matthew Henry, Matthew Henry Commentary on the Whole Bible (Complete). Vol. 1. N.p., 1706. http://www.biblestudytools.com/commentaries/matthew-henry-complete

invention of social media makes it really easy to publish everything you are thinking, experiencing and doing. I've never really understood sharing a photo of your meal!

Our challenge is how much we post on social media without it all being done for people to see. Sharing events to publicise is one thing but sharing every human interaction, every personal reflection from our time with Jesus perhaps leaves nothing as a secret, intimate conversation with him for the audience of One. In John 5:44, John repeats his point: "How can you believe if you accept praise from one another, yet make no effort to obtain the praise that comes from the only God?"[68] The words 'no effort' suggests something of being so distracted, so taken up with seeking praise from others that he suggests we might not even try to obtain praise and recognition from the Father.

RT Kendall writes, "**Can you imagine Jesus saying to the disciples after the Sermon on the Mount; 'How did I do? Was that not a pretty good sermon Peter?'**"[69] When I read that quote, I thought how ridiculous it was, of course Jesus wouldn't say that kind of thing. He wasn't insecure or needing reassurance like that and yet I know it is something I have often fallen into. I've told myself it's just getting some feedback when it has been about self-doubt.

So how do we get to a place where we are able to live solely for the praise and recognition of the Father? How

---

[68] Holy Bible, John 5:44, New International Version®, NIV® Copyright ©1973, 1978, 1984, 2011 by Biblica

[69] R.T Kendall, The Power of Humility, Charisma House, 2011, Pg 61

do we grow in security and identity, so we are free to serve selflessly and how do we find a place of wholeness that frees us from the weight of needing to find worth and security in whoever we meet?

Heart knowledge

I have always struggled with seeking praise and attention from others. I want people to like me, approve of me and to please others. In some senses, there isn't anything wrong with this: we all value encouragement, need relationship and affirmation; but it is what is behind this need that is the problem. For me, the need to be liked, approved of and to please others comes from a deficit in my own heart. The word NEED is important here. Do I NEED to be liked? Does it rock my identity and security if someone doesn't like me? Do I NEED to please others or is it nice to serve people well? If I need to please others, I will do whatever it takes, even if that means pulling people down, gossiping, doing things I wouldn't otherwise do so that I might please the person in front of me. This hunt and pursuit of security and approval is exhausting as we can never please everyone; we can never be liked by everyone and we can never be approved of by everyone. We will be left dissatisfied and disillusioned and insecure.

The moment of change and transformation for me came on a trip to Israel when I was nineteen years old. I had spent the day walking where Jesus had walked and in the evening our group got together to pray. As we prayed someone gave me the verse John 3:16. I thought it was nice and generic, but they explained that it stated 'God so loved the world' but when it said the world, it meant all humanity and as a part of all humanity it meant me too. That God so loves *me* that he gave... You see, I had grown up with a belief that God loved me in my head. I had been given the cheesy Christian stickers that had ended up on my illustrated Bible that said "God loves me" with a lovely picture of a teddy bear and a rainbow. You know the ones! If, as a child, you had asked me, "Does God love you?" I would have immediately, without flinching, said yes. It was exactly the same as when asked in what year was the Battle of Hastings: I would immediately recite 1066 without thought. I knew the right answer. It was stored in my head. However, the reality of the love of God had not made it to my heart. Spurgeon said, "That which is learned in the head may be unlearned, for our understanding is very fickle and our memory frail, but that which is written upon the heart cannot be erased."[70] Something happened that night in Bethlehem where I began to accept the love of God in my heart and to allow it to shape my character, my security and my identity.

Just as Jesus was spoken over by the Father at his baptism, we need to know that we are loved, accepted, valued by our Heavenly Father. For some of us, this is easier than it is for others, based on our experiences with our earthly fathers or significant authority figures in our lives. We must go on a journey of healing and deep heart

---

[70] Charles Spurgeon - https://www.spurgeon.org/resource-library/sermons/heart-knowledge-of-god/#flipbook/

revelation and discovery of the 'lavish love of God'.[71]

Part of the battle is identifying and having a sensitivity to our own insecurities. If we are blind to our insecurities, we can't work our way through them. Peter Scazzero says, "The vast majority of us go to our graves without knowing who we are."[72] This suggests that if we live from our insecurities, from the expectations of others or from our hurt or pain we end up living a wounded and distracted rather than whole and secure life. When we understand humility in this way, we can see insecurity in others as sad, frustrating and highlighting immaturity, as Murray suggests. Why would we want to keep on living like that?

Neil Anderson says, "Because wholeness and meaning in life are not the products of what you have or don't have, what you've done or haven't done. You are already a whole person and possess a life of infinite meaning and purpose because of who you are—a child of God."[73]

A Child first...

As a leader, I can be very driven. I've always been hard working and a doer and the challenge for me is to not be fixated on being a co-worker, co-labourer with Christ and

---

[71] Holy Bible, 1John 3:1, New International Version®, NIV® Copyright ©1973, 1978, 1984, 2011 by Biblica

[72] Peter Scazzero, Emotionally Healthy Spirituality, Zondervan, 2017

[73] Neil Anderson, Victory over the Darkness, Monarch Books, 2000, Pg 24

to try to earn God's love. Alternatively, I can try and seek approval from others by trying to do the best job I can while burning myself out, instead of allowing myself to be a child of God first. I need to let my identity be defined as a child of God, loved and whole and then my ministry, to my family and to the wider community to flow out of that. Scazzero helpfully asks this question on this point, "Is who you are determined by what you do, or is what you do determined by who you are?"[74] Finding a sense of worth through what we do is such an easy trap to fall into. It is important to remember how Jesus called his first disciples in Mark 3:14–15: "He appointed twelve that they might be with him and that he might send them out to preach and to have authority to drive out demons." [75]

We quickly focus on the doing, the preaching, being sent, authority etc., but miss the crucial bit: Jesus called them first to be with him. It is all about relationships before function. We are foolish if we forget this. Jesus invites us every day before we do anything for him, to simply be with him.

I've now been involved in the same ministry for twenty-three years and have been leading SWYM for eighteen years of that. It can be quite hard to separate, after all this time, what is me and what is my ministry. Whenever I step away for a retreat day, I might have a big agenda of what I really want God to speak to me about; and yet ninety-nine per cent of the time, God simply invites me to

---

[74] Peter Scazzero, Emotionally Healthy Spirituality, Zondervan, 2017

[75] Holy Bible, Mark 3:14-15, New International Version®, NIV® Copyright ©1973, 1978, 1984, 2011 by Biblica

remember that I am his child before anything else. It's where I remember that my security is found not in what I do, but who calls me their son; and that my identity is not my ministry, but my ministry flows out of my relationship. Neil Anderson describes it this way: "We don't serve God to gain His acceptance; we are accepted, so we serve God. We don't follow Him to be loved; we are loved, so we follow Him. It is not what we do that determines who we are; it is who we are that determines what we do." [76]

Jesus was wholly secure and lived for the praise and recognition of the Father and we are called to do the same. This requires receiving the acceptance and love of God for ourselves daily and to then to be in close communication with the Father, that we may be walking in obedience to Him. This is living for his praise and recognition. Spending our days listening to his instructions and guidance, so that we might make obedience to Him our chief aim rather than winning others to our cause or seeking their praise and respect. Again, Scazzero helpfully states, "The critical issue on the journey with God is not 'Am I happy?' but 'Am I free?'"[77]

Freedom can be found in knowing who we belong to and our security found in being a daughter or son of the maker of all things. Blanchard, Hodges and Hendry state: "When God is the source of your self-worth, you are no longer imprisoned by the pressure to do more and try

---

[76] Neil Anderson, Victory over the Darkness, Monarch Books, 2000

[77] Peter Scazzero, Emotionally Healthy Spirituality, Zondervan, 2017

harder. You can be a human being, not a human doing and you can relax in who God has made you to be." [78]

When we know who we are, we are free not just for freedom's sake but to serve others just as Christ served us. It's a life of modesty and of service. Kendall says, "We are called to modesty—that means we will do nothing to attract attention to ourselves. We will say nothing that makes us look good or would be self-vindicating. We should always let the other person praise us, making sure we are not eliciting praise. We should make every effort to get the praise that comes from God only.[79] "In essence, this is the challenge of living fully for God and not for others. Murray adds, "Humility towards men will be the only sufficient proof that our humility before God is real." [80]

This is really challenging. We can say we humble ourselves before God, but if we continue to live arrogantly and selfishly in front of others, we are deceiving ourselves. We must humble ourselves before God and then continue to humble ourselves before others, lowering ourselves to serve others just as Christ lowered Himself to serve us. Murray continues, "Our humility before God only has value inasmuch as it prepares us to reveal the humility of Jesus to our fellow

---

[78] Blanchard, Hodges and Hendry, Lead like Jesus Revisited, W Publishing, 2016

[79] R.T Kendall, The Power of Humility, Charisma House, 2011, Pg 63

[80] Andrew Murray, Humility – The Beauty of Holiness, Aneko Press, Revised Edition, 2016, Pg 31

man." [81] Living humbly before others begins to reveal Jesus to those around us and living humbly can only happen authentically as we place our value, our worth and our identity in God. Blanchard and Hodges summarise this neatly: "Humility is realising and emphasising the importance of other people. It is not putting yourself down; it is lifting others up. It is saying to yourself and to others 'I am precious in God's sight and so are you." [82]

Creating cultures that pursue wholeness not driven insecurity

The challenge of leading a group of people in whatever context is that people are complicated. They are a wonderfully weird mix of strengths, personalities, hang-ups, hurts and successes. If we are honest, we are all a bit messed up and can react and spark off each other in the wrong environment or setting. So, how do we try to lead and set a culture where we encourage and accept people as they are and challenge them to be more whole whilst not pressurising people and making them feel more insecure?

Jesus managed to create an inner team of twelve who belonged and who all were allowed to be themselves. They were brought together from such a variety of

---

[81] Andrew Murray, Humility – The Beauty of Holiness, Aneko Press, Revised Edition, 2016, Pg 33

[82] Ken Blanchard and Phil Hodges, Lead like Jesus: Lessons from the Greatest Leadership role model of all time, Nashville, 2005, Pg 67

backgrounds and yet Jesus wasn't afraid to pull them up when they were getting it wrong. He was fierce in his pursuit of their humility and encouraged them to not seek praise from man.

Jesus was practical, deliberate, prophetic and provocative and formed a team seeking to follow in his model. Franz Grillparzer challengingly said, "To test a modest man's modesty do not investigate if he ignores applause; find out if he abides criticism."[83] As leaders, our reaction to criticism should show us how secure we really are. Do we get defensive, sound off or some other reaction that highlights a deeper woundedness than the criticism alone? If we react defensively, we cannot expect our teams to be any different when we have given them feedback, we have given them permission to do the same as us. Instead, we must take our pain, our woundedness, to God our Healer and seek his restoration.

Whether intentional or not, we set team cultures. And what we allow/celebrate/laugh at/ignore all helps create a culture. We can create a culture of wholeness and humility if we intentionally model, guard and pursue it as a group. But how do we do this? Here are a few key principles:

1. **When creating teams, look first for teachable hearts over giftedness:** You can train someone how to do something if they are teachable. What is teachability? Being teachable is to be ready and willing to learn and grow, recognising you can learn

---

[83] Franz Grillparzer -https://www.azquotes.com/author/5936-Franz_Grillparzer/tag/criticism

from any and everyone and seeking to humble yourself daily. As we look to add to our team, the temptation we face is to add the qualified, the experienced and the gifted, but the first thing should be to be humble and teachable. We need them to have a sense of calling to this area of service and we want them to have good chemistry with the rest of the team and be competent people who can do the role, but first must come character. I am fortunate to have a team at SWYM that embodies this. It is a pleasure to lead the team and there is humility and a teachability that means we can have robust conversations and difference of agreement, but we choose to submit to each other. This is a gift, but you must fiercely fight for it. Over the years, whenever I've sensed people fighting for position, competing or getting defensive, I've had to call it out and address it individually and sometimes all together. Even if you have a teachable team, you still have to guard it with all you have. But what if you have inherited a team? What if they were not your choice and you can't get rid of them? The truth is that when we inherit a team, we have to get the wrong people off the bus and the right people on to it. Sometimes, this is managing people carefully and lovingly on to something else. (This is no easy task to do and avoid hurt in the process—do not rush it.) If there are one or more individuals who don't want to move on and it feels like these people are going against the kind of humble culture you want to create, then try one or all of the following points.

2. **Prioritise space for prayer/worship as a team:** Creating space to open the Bible, worship in whatever style is your tradition and pray together will help to soften people's hearts. As a team, we gather both online and, in the office, so that everyone who is free can join in every morning for thirty minutes from 9am to pray. It is a space to remind ourselves that everything we do individually or as a team starts with our relationship with Jesus and it all belongs to him. Whenever we gather as a team for a meeting, we have space to pray, sing or read the Bible or to receive prayer. As leaders, it is important to be vulnerable in these spaces, as it gives permission for anyone else to be struggling or battling with something. Create a space for God to speak, soften hearts and build a culture of thanksgiving and vulnerability. This space regularly reminds us about where our identity and security comes from. This culture setting can help to form a more humble, others-focused environment. However, don't be fooled that simply having a prayer meeting will solve all your problems. We must guard and fight fiercely for humility in these spaces as leaders.

3. **Encouragement and affirmation:** It is now widely known that in management we should seek to give an 'encouragement sandwich'. In other words, we should praise before and after challenging someone. We all know that we need more encouragement than criticism and yet we know how quick we can be to point out others' mistakes. People are much more likely to receive criticism well and change practice if they are in an

encouraging, affirming environment. If we feel safe, we are able to trust what others are saying and take it on board. As leaders, do we take time to think about how we might encourage our team? Have we learnt how our team value encouragement? It is a good challenge to try and create a culture where everyone is secure enough in themselves that they have a sincere desire to build up and encourage each other. The day when you, as a leader, can step back and say, 'They are doing it without me instigating it,' is a good day. We need to make sure the encouragement and affirmation we give is meaningful and heartfelt. Is it something that was appreciated and valued? Is it just lip service or genuine appreciation? We need to make sure that we don't create a culture that feeds those seeking approval. Occasionally, when teams are large, some individuals don't receive praise or encouragement from others, unless it is given from the pastor/minister/leaders in your context. The challenge is not withholding praise when it is due, but to look for settings to gently challenge and encourage the individual to be pursuing the praise and recognition of the Father, not of the leaders.

4. **Honest conversation—tackle issues as they appear**: Part of fierce humility is about fighting for humility in our team. It is important to say that this means we cannot be conflict avoiders and hope issues go away. Dallas Willard said, "The alternative course of indecision and non-confrontation proves highly costly in the long term, to those who are led as much as to their leader...In some churches...there is so much metaphorical dust swept under the

carpet that the carpet lies three foot off the ground!"[84] Jesus spoke up, confronted and restored his team; he did not sweep anything under the carpet, he took the costly but fruitful route. Fierce humility, however, is not an excuse to bully, tear down or criticise those in our team. If we are in a position of leadership, it is our role if following in the way of Jesus to be serving and lovingly lowering ourselves for our team. We address issues when they arise, not to score points or to establish our authority, but for the development and the wholeness of those on our team. We don't allow unspoken issues to stack up and we also choose our battles and learn to lovingly correct, challenge and re-establish culture. For far too long, leadership has been used to abuse, manipulate and control. Men have been especially prone to this, so if you are a man reading this, can I encourage you to choose your battles and to reflect and learn how to correct in a kind, releasing loving way? There is a balance to be found regarding conflict and we will return to this later, but my philosophy has always been that I would rather be known for having been gracious than having been cruel. That does not mean I am a pushover but that when I challenge, I try and do it in a gracious, kind way. If someone has a splinter in their arm, they can ignore it and be in pain, but it could eventually become infected and cause bigger issues. To help this person, you could carefully and lovingly tease it out with minimal fuss leaving the recipient grateful and better. Alternatively,

---

[84] Dallas Willard, Renovation of the Heart, SPCK, 2021

you could get a knife and cut out a chunk of their skin without their permission, attacking their arm to remove the splinter by force. This leaves the recipient attacked, invaded and wounded. It is an outrageous example, but something I'm sure we can relate to when it comes to someone raising an issue with us in a harsh and overbearing way, or when we know we have gone in too strong to resolve something and in the end made things worse.

The start of our journey towards fierce humility is learning to live for the praise and recognition of the Father not the crowd. This is something we must walk towards and fight for in our teams. Ministry that flows out of an identity and security found in Christ is much more likely to be healthy and produce fruit that lasts. If we are serving out of our own woundedness we are much more likely to wound others and therefore part of the fight for fierce humility is about breaking cycles of hurt and walking towards healing and wholeness. The next challenge is not to serve in our own strength but to rely fully on His; however, before we turn to this, let's take a moment to pause and reflect on the prayer and questions below.

Pause | Selah

"Lord, help me to be still before you. Lead me to a greater vision of who you are and in so doing, may I see myself—the good, the bad and the ugly. Grant me the courage to follow you, to be faithful, to become the unique person you have created me to be. I ask you for the Holy Spirit's power to not copy another person's life or journey. 'God, submerge me in the darkness of your love, that the consciousness of my false, everyday self falls away from [me] like a soiled garment ... May my deep self fall into your presence ... knowing you alone ... carried away into eternity like a dead leaf in the November wind.' In Jesus' name, Amen."[85]

---

[85] Peter Scazzero, Emotionally Healthy Spirituality, Zondervan, 2017

Questions for discussion/reflection

1. Can you identify anyone who you work hard to impress or whose approval you crave? If so, why?

2. When is your security and identity in Christ challenged? What does a wholly secure you look like? What does an insecure you look like?

3. When have you seen conflict handled badly in a team? What made it bad? When have you seen conflict handled really well? What made it good?

4. What one step can you make today to create a more humble, wholly secure team environment?

If we can believe that God is who He says He is and therefore trust Him with every facet of our lives, then we can simply enjoy walking life with God.

Chapter 3
Fiercely Relying on the Father, Not on Own Strength or Gifting

"Swallowing your pride seldom leads to indigestion."[86]

"My grace is sufficient for you, for my power is made perfect in weakness."

2 Corinthians 12:9[87]

For the first few years of SWYM's journey, we had used a former vicarage in Exeter as an office base. We started with just three desks in what would have been the living room of the house. Over the years, as things grew, we gradually took over more of the house until it was all office space. Then, after almost fifteen years, it reached the point where we had outgrown it. At various moments, I had tried to find something else, keeping an eye out for office spaces or trying to figure out a way we could get more space. But nothing seemed to be the right fit. It was as if I was trying to push a boulder uphill; nothing was happening. In the end, I felt I needed to lay it down and not try sorting it in my own strength.

A few months later, I remember calling one of our team from a summer festival where I had found a canvas print of the following verse: "Now to him who is able to do

---

[86] Author unknown

[87] Holy Bible, 2 Cor 12 v 9, New International Version®, NIV® Copyright ©1973, 1978, 1984, 2011 by Biblica

immeasurably more than all we ask or imagine." [88] The verse had been significant for us in SWYM over the years. There were two different sizes of canvas, one that was quite small but would fit nicely in the current office and a larger print that wouldn't fit in the current office but could potentially fit in a bigger office. It felt like it was a moment of taking a small step of faith and trust. So, I bought the bigger canvas with the view that if a new space became available, we would place it in the new office; I would leave it with God until then.

I came back after some time off—six months later—with a sense from God that now was the time. I was still aware this could just be me so tried to just let God lead the process rather than trying to force something to happen. We went to see a warehouse unit that came up for sale. It was perfect: predominantly office space, it had space for storage and being situated out of the city, was easy for people to get to. I was excited but aware that we had no money to buy it. I spoke to the estate agent who said they had already had an asking price offer for the warehouse but that the buyers were going to need some time to get the money together. If we could make a cash offer at the asking price in the next fortnight the place was ours. I said to the estate agent that I didn't think I'd be in touch as we simply didn't have any money.

We reached out to five or six of our supporters and friends to ask them to pray and, amazingly, within forty-eight hours, we had the two-hundred thousand pounds we needed to buy the warehouse. A large amount of this

---

[88] Holy Bible, Ephesians 3:10, Holy Bible, Ephesians 3 v 10, New International Version®, NIV® Copyright ©1973, 1978, 1984, 2011 by Biblica

was through interest free loans but we decided to go ahead (as it felt right to the Holy Spirit and to us) and over the next four months before we got the keys, we had received all the money in full—plus an extra fifty-thousand pounds to make the space fit for purpose. Individuals and trusts had been so generous, which meant we owned the warehouse outright with no debt at all. When it was the right moment, it was the right moment. It was a lesson learned for me: when God is doing something we just get out of the way and let him do it rather than trying to force something to happen in our own strength at the wrong time. I've never experienced in such a quick and categoric way the provision and intervention of God. I could genuinely say I just rode the wave of God opening the door and providing everything we needed. It was an amazing experience!

As leaders, we often start out in roles where the idea of doing it in our own strength seems a totally alien concept. We step out nervously into each new task and responsibility with a desperate dependence on God for each thing. But as we grow in confidence, experience and opportunity we can get complacent and start to rely on our own ability and gifts. In my experience, it can be a very gradual process of complacency; in our busyness we just crack on and it's only afterwards we recognise that we did it without Him. For me practically, this can look like recognition that I didn't pray before I stepped into that meeting or before that talk. Or, I didn't have an ongoing listening conversation with Jesus through the event or day but had my head down and was doing my "job". It's when dependency becomes complacency! Murray said, "Humility, the place of entire dependence on God, is the first duty of the creature and the root of every good quality."[89] It is that dependence on God that we must seek if we want to walk in humility and operate in God's strength not our own.

Nothing

Jesus modelled a life dependant on the Father. When teaching the disciples in John 15, he speaks of the vine and the branches and encourages them and us to remain in Him. In verse four and five, Jesus says:

Remain in me, as I also in you. No branch can bear fruit by itself; it must remain in the vine. Neither can you bear fruit unless you remain in me.

I am the vine; you are the branches. If you remain in me and I in you, you will bear much fruit; apart from me you can do nothing.[90]

Nothing! Apart from me, you can do nothing! No transformation, no Kingdom impact, no lasting change. We cannot bear fruit ourselves. We are unable to do it. We must be grafted into the vine and be branches with the lifeblood of Christ flowing through us producing the fruit. We do not force fruit to come, we do not strive, but we allow God to grow the fruit as we focus on remaining in Him.

---

[89] Andrew Murray, Humility – The Beauty of Holiness, Aneko Press, Revised Edition, 2016, Pg 2

[90] Holy Bible, John 15:4–5, New International Version®, NIV® Copyright ©1973, 1978, 1984, 2011 by Biblica

Remaining or abiding in Jesus, William Barclay states, 'will mean arranging life, arranging prayer, arranging silence in such a way that there is never a day when we give ourselves a chance to forget him.'[91] If we can do nothing without Him, we must learn how to do everything with him.

Jesus doesn't ask us to do something he isn't willing to do himself. He models to us what it is to do this. In John 5:19–20, in response to the Jewish leaders persecuting him, Jesus says:

Very truly I tell you, the Son can do nothing by himself; he can do only what he sees his Father doing, because whatever the Father does the Son also does. For the Father loves the Son and shows him all he does. Yes and he will show him even greater works than these, so that you will be amazed. [92]

Once again, that word "nothing" appears. Jesus says He, too, can do nothing by himself. He has the same restrictions, the same challenge as us: to live our lives totally dependent on the Father. He describes only being able to do what He sees the Father doing. Jesus models to us that we must surrender, we must submit to God and must place all our trust and hope in Him. Horne, when reflecting on this topic, wrote, "In the spiritual war, in which we are all engaged, the first and necessary step to victory is, to renounce all confidence in the wisdom and

---

[91] William Barclay, The Gospel of John: Volume 2, Westminster John Knox Press, 2001

[92] John 5:19–20, New International Version®, NIV® Copyright ©1973, 1978, 1984, 2011 by Biblica

strength of nature and the world; and to remember, that we can do nothing, but in the name, by the merits, through the power and for the sake of Jesus Christ, our Lord and our God." [93] Life, ministry and service must, for us, be through the power and authority of Jesus; for the fame and the praise of Jesus alone.

Andrew Murray adds, "The root of all goodness and grace, of all faith and acceptable worship, is that we know we have nothing but what we receive and bow in deepest humility to wait upon God for it." [94] Knowing we have nothing but what we receive, nothing of ourselves to offer but our bodies as living sacrifices (Romans 12:1), that we can do nothing apart from Jesus is to humble ourselves. To depend on God is to live lower, to be available to Him by dying to ourselves.

When I was in my late teens and early twenties, I was, unashamedly, a huge fan of Christian rock music. I still have a vast collection of albums on my devices from the late 90s but one quiet, reflective song from the band 'The Waiting' has always disturbed and challenged me. In the chorus they sang, "Make it disappear, everything I've built with my hands, make it disappear, kick it over like a castle of sand 'til nothing stands ... **Let my kingdom fall. Every castle, every wall."**[95]

---

[93] Thomas Horne, https://thestevenobleshow.com/2023/03/20/what-are-you-trusting-in-psalm-20/

[94] Andrew Murray, Humility – The Beauty of Holiness, Aneko Press, Revised Edition, 2016, Pg 17

[95] The Waiting, Unfazed, Make it Disappear, Track 6, 1998

I was disturbed as I reflected on that song as I started out in full-time ministry but, perhaps, even more so twenty-five years later. What if God did make everything I've built with my hands disappear? What if God did kick it over like a castle of sand? Would there be much left? The final challenge— "Let my Kingdom fall, every castle, every wall"—has remained a challenge through all these years. I do not want to build any kind of empire of my own, I want to build His Kingdom.

Emma Ineson speaks of ambition when she writes, "The key to developing godly ambition is to keep an eye on our motivations. Now, as human beings, we will not always be able easily to divide the good from the sinful in terms of motivation for ambition. There is likely to be a messy, human muddle between the two, but my guess is that we know when we are seeking promotion in order to validate ourselves or find significance we lack elsewhere. These are the moments to check in with our motivations and our reasons for doing what we do."[96] We build our own kingdoms when our need for significance, success and promotion trumps being obedient children.

Humility is the only way to build His Kingdom. Bonhoeffer summarises this well when he wrote, "It is not we who build. He wills to build the church. No man builds the church but Christ alone. Whoever is minded to build the church is surely well on the way to destroying it; for he will build a temple to idols without wishing or knowing it. We must confess—he builds. We must proclaim—he

---

[96] Emma Ineson, Ambition, spck, 2019, pg 34

builds. We must pray to Him—he builds."[97] It is all about Jesus. Without Him we can do nothing, we can build nothing, everything will disappear that is done in our own strength.

It is important to remember that although I can do nothing without Jesus, I "can do all things through him who gives me strength'[98] and nothing will be impossible with God".[99] For as the canvas displayed proudly on the wall of our new warehouse office reminds us, "Now to him who is able to do immeasurably more than all we ask or imagine, according to his power that is at work within us, to him be glory in the church and in Christ Jesus throughout all generations, for ever and ever! Amen!"[100]

This whole point of trust, dependence and obedience is so helpfully portrayed by Simon Peter in Luke 5:4–5 as Jesus instructs him to 'put out into deep water and let down the nets for a catch.'[101] Peter knew what he was doing, this was not something new for him. He knew these waters; he knew his trade. He could have

---

[97] Church Election Sermon Preached by Pr. Dietrich Bonhoeffer, July 23, 1933 at Trinity Church in Berlin.

[98] Holy Bible, Philippians 4:13 New International Version®, NIV® Copyright ©1973, 1978, 1984, 2011 by Biblica

[99] Holy Bible, Luke 1:37 New International Version®, NIV® Copyright ©1973, 1978, 1984, 2011 by Biblica

[100] Holy Bible, Ephesians 3:20-21 New International Version®, NIV® Copyright ©1973, 1978, 1984, 2011 by Biblica

[101] Holy Bible, Luke 5:4-5 New International Version®, NIV® Copyright ©1973, 1978, 1984, 2011 by Biblica

questioned what this carpenter, this Rabbi might know about fishing. His response, though, is beautiful: "Master, we've worked hard all night and haven't caught anything. But because you say so, I will let down the nets." He had caught NOTHING—and yet as he listened, as he depended on and obeyed Jesus everything changed. It is all about dependence and trust in spite of what we might be thinking or feeling.

Trusting God

I know that, given the opportunity, I can be a bit of a control freak. I like to be involved in projects and tasks. I like to be able to make sure things happen well and that everything has been covered. The problem is that it can have a big effect on my walk with God because when it comes down to my life, I want to be in control and want to fix things and generally control what is happening around me.

A few years ago, whilst on holiday, I read two books. The first was the life story of Hudson Taylor, who formed a missionary society to China and the second, the life story of George Muller, who formed children's homes in Bristol. I was inspired by the same features of these two men: they trusted God and they believed God could do anything. George Muller never asked for money but created homes for one thousand children at a time. He fed, watered, cared for and employed staff whilst never asking for money. Taylor developed a strategy to reach the whole of China for Jesus and he constantly relied on God financially, for safety and for all his daily decisions.

Both men were world changers; these men were people of prayer. Both men walked with God. As I read these two books, I was amazed as I saw these men daily committing their lives and the things that mattered that day, the people around them and their finances and health to God and making a choice to trust God with these things. They trusted God with everything and lived dependant on him for everything.

As I've reflected on this, I'm making a choice to follow in their footsteps with renewed determination. You know what? It is liberating! If we can believe that God is who He says He is and therefore trust Him with every facet of our lives, then we can simply enjoy walking life with God. We will suddenly find opportunities to see God at work rather than trying to sort out every problem in our lives ourselves, getting stressed and anxious and disappointed in the process. If I can believe that God is Jehovah Jireh and will provide for me as I put Him and His Kingdom first, I can relax about my finances. If I can believe that God is Jehovah Shammah, meaning God who is Present, I don't have to worry about feeling God's presence all the time, I can trust that He is there. If I can believe that God is Yahweh Mekoddishkem, God our sanctifier, then I can trust that he will make me like Jesus.

The question is: How much do we really trust God? Solomon wrote in Proverbs 3-5, "Trust in the Lord with all your heart and lean not on your own understanding."[102] In other words, completely Trust God with everything you hold dear. He is God after all. Brother Lawrence wrote,

---

[102] Holy Bible, Proverbs 3:5, New International Version®, NIV® Copyright ©1973, 1978, 1984, 2011 by Biblica

"We should put life in our faith. We should give ourselves utterly to God in pure abandonment, in temporal and spiritual matters alike and find contentment in the doing of His will, whether he takes us through sufferings or consolations."[103]

Pure abandonment in everything is real trust. It is dependence upon and trust in God. When we think about this, there can be a sense of risk about this way of life. And, yet it is always good to remember that God is the safest place to place our trust. The one who is faithful, trustworthy, our rock and place of safety, the Almighty King of Kings, who holds all authority. Anywhere else is second best and risky, whether the stock exchange, housing market, our own energy and effort and fight, or our families and friends. All of these can and will let us down, but there is one who will never let us down. It is easy to know in our heads that we need to trust God but to live it is one of life's biggest challenges in my experience.

Leading a charity is a huge privilege. I love my job and am aware that many people don't have that joy. I've led a local church and a regional charity and there are different challenges and frustrations in both. One area I have found consistently challenging in leading a charity is finance and managing budgets. You might be reading this involved in church leadership and saying that it is the same issue for you. My experience with a church is at least you had a crowd of people who were consistently giving and who you could appeal to if things were tight.

---

[103] Brother Lawrence, The Practice of the Presence of God, Hodder & Stoughton, 1981, Pg 20

With SWYM, however, our budget was significantly bigger with more staff but also with year-by-year guessing games on what we might get in through churches and trainees, grants and random gifts. Our financial year-end is the end of August, which means that for the last eighteen years, between April-August, we start preparing the following year's budget. This is always a time of uncertainty. Each year, the budget looks pretty depressing as we submit it to trustees as a first draft in July. I don't remember a year when we had a positive budget at this point. However, throughout the last eighteen years, God has somehow always provided as we have put our trust in Him. Yes, occasionally, we have had to make difficult decisions but, somehow and often I have no clue how, we have come through and come through well.

The inner battle during this period is hard. I feel the weight of the world on my shoulders as I consider the staff and their families and want to cover their salaries in the budget as well as all the projects and plans we have for the coming year. I have moments of self-doubt around some of the decisions we've made. For example: Have we overstretched ourselves? Have we been unwise? I have been hugely encouraged to have a treasurer walking this with me over this whole time who has a brilliant mix of wisdom and faith. I can remember him saying to me many times, "How are we stepping out in faith this year?" Or "God has always taken care of us before; I'm really relaxed as I know He will again." Internally, it is a daily battle of doing all I can to help make things balance financially but then, stopping and trusting and waiting on God. I'm not very good at that waiting part, if I'm honest. I'm very impatient but I've learned that it is in the waiting that God forms our character.

There is a famous saying that some attribute to Augustine and some to Ignatius, which says, "Pray as though everything depended on God; act as though everything depended on you." At first glance I agree with this quote as it forces me to get on my knees and pray and to also do my bit but the more I reflect on it the more I think it isn't quite right. If we act as if it all depends on us, will that not create a desperate workaholic nature that ultimately makes us try to do it in our own strength? Although there is some disagreement about where the quote comes from, there is a helpful and I'd suggest more well-rounded, quote found in Pedro de Ribadeneira's biography of Ignatius where it says, "In matters which he took up pertaining to the service of our Lord, he made use of all the human means to succeed in them, with a care and efficiency as great as if the success depended on these means; and he confided in God and depended on his providence as greatly as if all the other human means which he was using were of no effect."[104]

This quote perhaps adds more detail but still leaves some room for debate. Ultimately, we must not be lazy and sit on our hands waiting for God to act on our behalf whilst doing nothing. But similarly, I don't believe that 'God helps those who help themselves,'[105] and I do believe that a drivenness or striving is unhelpful when it comes to trust and dependence. As we look at the life of Jesus, we

---

[104] Pedro de Ribadeneira, The Life of Ignatius of Loyola, 2014

[105] Benjamin Franklin, Poor Richard's Almorac, 1757

see him partnering with the Father; he had to reach out to heal, open his mouth to teach, ask the disciples to follow. He was absolutely involved in all he achieved for the Father but he was dependant on and directed by the Father. He didn't strive, apart from to do the Father's will. He wasn't driven other than towards the Cross. A balance, then, must be found between participation with and dependence upon God; but a balance is hard to find in my experience. Therefore, I believe it best as John Sammis put it so well:

Trust and obey, for there's no other way. To be happy in Jesus, but to trust and obey

Not a shadow can rise, not a cloud in the skies, But His smile quickly drives it away. Not a doubt or a fear, not a sigh or a tear. Can abide while we trust and obey

Trust and obey, for there's no other way. To be happy in Jesus, but to trust and obey.[106]

Jesus both taught about and modelled living in dependence on God and not operating out of your own strength. In fact, he fiercely pursued this kind of life for his disciples. When they returned with joy from being sent out in Luke 10:17 they said, "Lord, even the demons submit to us in your name."[107] Take note, that they said submit to us, a danger they might think they can do this in their own strength although "in your name" is a good recognition that it is because of Jesus that they are

---

[106] John Sammis, Trust and Obey, 1887

[107] Holy Bible, Luke 10:17, New International Version®, NIV® Copyright ©1973, 1978, 1984, 2011 by Biblica

submitting. Jesus replied, "Do not rejoice that the spirits submit to you but rejoice that your names are written in heaven." In other words, rejoice in what God has done for you not what you have done for God. Jesus knows that even when doing things in His name, we are likely to succumb to pride. He wants his disciples to be fiercely humble so they might be used more fully by God in his service.

What then can we do in our teams and leadership to fiercely guard humility in this area?

1. **Model it ourselves:** We must not ask our teams to go where we are not prepared to go ourselves. We will influence the culture of our team by seeking every day to fully depend on God in all that we are doing. As we model this and turn away from self-dependency, it can become contagious. People recognising they too can trust and pray and not be driven. That they too can do their best and leave the rest with God.

2. **More Prayer less Panic:** One way we can fiercely guard this way of Jesus is to pray more and panic less. Often, the times when we want to depend on ourselves are when things are stressful and overwhelming; in these moments calling our team to prayer is a great way to keep calling everyone back to dependence. A few years ago, I decided that whenever I had a meeting with anyone, I would always pray with them. I didn't want this to be a religious act but a reminder to me that this was about God's work not mine. I wanted to acknowledge that this ministry was his ministry, not mine and that even if I had an agenda for what I

wanted to come out of this meeting, that I submitted to His plans and purposes. Praying was for my heart's benefit and to hopefully bless the other. In my own strength, I could easily try to push my own will through in meetings whereas in God's strength I was seeking God's will to be done. What I found, however, was that by my choice to always pray inadvertently impacted those I was with and I noticed others started to do the same. We can fiercely protect this way of being and working by calling out when our team are stressed and panicked and leading them in prayer and laying these things down.

It's important to say, that it is important not to do this in an annoying over-spiritual way. Sometimes, people are stressed because if they don't get this task done, then things won't happen or will be unsafe. Calling a prayer meeting for half an hour at this moment might add to their stress, so asking the rest of the team to pray for them whilst they carry on working—or just leading a short prayer with them to give it back to Jesus—is much more releasing and helpful. We need to create some habits for humility; habits that draw us back to prayer and letting go so God can achieve what he wants to achieve through us. Habits could include stopping at midday to pray, starting the day right as a team, meeting to worship and pray. Habits could include gathering as a team to submit our plans to Him before sending off a proposal. Habits for humility will always draw us back to prayer and away from panic.

3. **Stepping out in faith into the uncomfortable spaces:** Nothing breeds trust and dependence more than being out of our depth. The reason we grow in

self-dependence and complacency is that we become too comfortable. Andrew Murray wrote, "The absence of humility is the secret cause of why the power of God cannot do it's mighty work".[108] If we do ministry in our strength, we stop God from being able to move. So, what do we need to do? I'm reminded again of our treasurer saying, "How are we going to step out in faith this year?" It's a good question to ask. Where are we stepping out? Where, if God doesn't show up, will it completely fail. Michelangelo famously said, "The greatest danger for most of us is not that our aim is too high and we miss it, but that it is too low and we reach it."[109] So, firstly for ourselves, we must shake off complacency and set what Jim Collins calls BHAGS: Big Hairy Audacious Goals[110]. That means finding some God-inspired, faith-stretching goals that force us to depend on God, for without Him it could never happen. It's amazing how desperation drives us to our knees, but ease draws us to distraction.

Jesus was fiercely focused on humbling himself by living dependant on his Father and teaching his disciples to do the same. Before we move on to explore how this dependence is only really possible through fiercely pursuing time with the Father, let us pause and reflect on our own or with our team on what this dependence and trust might look like for us in our individual settings.

---

[108] Andrew Murray, Humility – The Beauty of Holiness, Aneko Press, Revised Edition, 2016, Pg 30

[109] Michelangelo - https://sites.google.com/a/ccpsnet.net/english-10-survival-site/home/essay-prompt-pages/quote-based-essay-prompts/michelangelo-quote-prompt

[110] James Collins, Good to Great, Harper Collins Publishers Inc, 2001

Pause | Selah

It is no good giving me a play like Hamlet or King Lear,

and telling me to write a play like that. Shakespeare could do it; I can't

And it is no good showing me a life like Jesus and telling me to live a life like that.

Jesus could do it; but I can't.

But if the genius of Shakespeare could come and live in me,

then I could write plays like his.

And if the Spirit of Jesus could come and live in me,

then I could live a life like his.[111]

William Temple

---

[111] William Temple, quoted in The Radical Disciple, John Stott, ivp, 2010, Pg 40

Questions for reflection/discussion

1. What are you struggling to fully Trust God with right now in your own personal life and in your leadership?

2. What does dependence upon God need to look more like practically for you?

3. As a team, what does more prayer, less panic look like for you?

4. As a team, where is God calling you out in faith into the uncomfortable spaces?

> *Seeking encounter not religious activity is what makes the difference,*

Chapter 4
Fiercely Seeking Time Alone With the Father

"Jesus constantly taught, exhorted, encouraged and inspired his disciples to pray. Prayer was the breath he breathed, the driving force of his life, the secret of his astonishing ministry."
David Watson[112]

"Teach us to pray."
Luke 11:11[113]

From a young age, I knew that spending time with God on your own was something that was good for you. I saw my mum reading her Bible in the kitchen most days. She regularly bought me devotional magazines to encourage me to do the same, which I occasionally read! I remember seeing my dad's open Bible in his study in amongst all the farming paperwork and files. The Bible was an open book in our house and I didn't realise until much later what a huge privilege that was for me.

I can remember walking into my parents' bedroom early in the morning or late at night and seeing my dad

---

[112] David Watson, Called and Committed: World Changing Discipleship, Crown Publishing Group, Pg 82

[113] Holy Bible, Luke 11:11, New International Version®, NIV® Copyright ©1973, 1978, 1984, 2011 by Biblica

kneeling at the foot of the bed and praying. I didn't really know how long he stayed there for, but I knew he was talking and listening to God, so I would back out of the room to give him some space.

I grew up on a farm on the edge of Exmoor National Park in North Devon. It is a beautiful part of the world and I have lots of happy memories of walking through the fields of our farm, spending time with God, often wearing headphones listening to Christian music and occasionally singing out lyrics at the top of my voice for all the cows to hear! Although a lot of my mountaintop spiritual experiences took place in large crowds at Christian festivals, camps and events, the truth is that the place where I most frequently heard the voice of God was in the quiet. Moments of clarity about next steps, moments of peace and moments of rest in his presence were profound just all on my own.

I am a massive extrovert! My Myers Briggs 'E' score was off the chart. I really do get my energy from being with other people and find lots of time on my own—not very good for my soul, but I learnt in those early days of faith, living in the middle of nowhere, that God could be found in the quiet lonely places. I discovered that my favourite place to spend time with God was in creation where I would be inspired by a tree, a cloud, a bird or a leaf.

I have recently moved with my family to a rural part of mid-Devon and I've loved nothing more than late night walks on the lanes or daytime strolls looking out over green hills inspiring me to worship and to be still. As I get older, the responsibilities I've added from family and wider ministry means that there is always a fight for my attention and, therefore, the need to find that quiet place with God is even more necessary. There have been seasons when finding space to seek God has been incredibly hard; there have been seasons when spending time with God has felt dry and stale; there have been seasons when I avoided spending time with Him; and there have been seasons when I couldn't do anything when I came before Him but simply just to 'be'. I know that time with the Father is what I need but sometimes life gets in the way.

As leaders, we know before we do anything for Him we are called to be with him, but often the demands of others squeezes out quality time with God. We can end up pretending that everything is wonderful in our personal walk when we feel as dry as a bone. Ruth Haley Barton writes, "Without the regular experience of being received and loved by God in solitude and silence, we are vulnerable to a kind of leadership that is driven by profound emptiness that we are seeking to fill through performance and achievement."[114] If most of us are honest, we can all relate from our own experience at one point or another feeling like we are operating out of a profound emptiness.

This emptiness might be as a result of tiredness, burnout or a feeling of disconnection from God. In these times, we can act as if we have just come out of an hour lost in wonder, love and praise when actually, we overslept after a late meeting the night before and have said a quick "Hello" to God as we jumped into our first meeting of the

---

[114] Ruth Haley Barton, Strengthening the Soul of your Leadership, IVP, 2018, Pg 126

day. I've certainly had times when I've come to God and it feels so rushed that it doesn't feel like quality time at all.

There is always the danger that we spend all our time with God with others being present that we don't really know how to be alone with Him anymore. Ruth Barton helpfully challenges us all when she says, "Silence and solitude bring us face to face with our addiction to being in control, there is also an invitation to let go and allow God to be in control."[115] We don't seek God's presence just to address our issues but as we encounter Him, we become more aware of our fallenness and need of Him in everything. Andrew Murray adds, "The creature must accept that its main concern, its best asset, its only happiness, now and through all eternity, is to present itself an empty vessel in which God can dwell and demonstrate His power and goodness."[116] Spending time with our Father is what enables us to find humility, as we empty ourselves and ask God to fill us again. Murray continues, "All external teaching and personal effort is ineffective to conquer pride or produce the meek and lowly heart...It is only by the indwelling of Christ, His divine humility that we become truly humble."[117] Here we see that humility is not earned or achieved but is a gift that is given as we allow Jesus to fill us with his humility as we spend time with Him.

---

[115] Ruth Haley Barton, Invitation to Solitude and Silence, SPCK, 2021

[116] Andrew Murray, Humility – The Beauty of Holiness, Aneko Press, Revised Edition, 2016, Pg 27

[117] Andrew Murray, Humility – The Beauty of Holiness, Aneko Press, Revised Edition, 2016, Pg 27

Wherever you are currently in this area of personal pursuit of time with God, this chapter is not about making you feel guilty so you do more or try to be better. Far from it! But my hope is that it is an honest conversation on a topic we all know is so crucial to our lives. How do we then fiercely and humbly pursue time with the Father?

Jesus, as our chief example, took time out regularly to be alone to seek his Father. Each one of the Gospel writers tells us 'Jesus often withdrew to lonely places and prayed'[118], or words to that effect. The fact that all the Gospels mention Jesus spending time alone with the Father tells us that they felt it was significant for readers to know.

That word 'often' is significant: this was not just for special occasions but was part of a rhythm of prayer that Jesus inhabited. Jesus modelled what it looks like to seek the Father and he took time out during the busiest, as well as the saddest, moments of his ministry. Dallas Willard comments, "It was in his 'tent of meeting' in the solitary place, 'in my Father's house' (Luke 2:49) that Jesus' character was developed and his unique accessibility forged."[119] Here, we see Jesus' fierce pursuit of the Father led to a unique accessibility that enabled him to always do the Father's will.

Having established that Jesus 'often withdrew' in Luke 5, Luke, a chapter later, describes a time when 'Jesus went out to a mountainside to pray and spent the night praying

---

[118] Holy Bible, Luke 5:6, New International Version®, NIV® Copyright ©1973, 1978, 1984, 2011 by Biblica

[119] Dallas Willard, Renovation of the Heart, SPCK, 2021

to God.'[120] After that night of prayer, Jesus chose 'the twelve'. That night of prayer seems to be a specific and extended time, seeking discernment regarding this important decision. Matthew, Mark and John describe Jesus walking on water and draw our attention to the fact that before this, Jesus went by himself to a mountainside to pray. John helpfully gives some additional context that, "Jesus, knowing that the crowd intended to come and make him king by force, withdrew again."[121] Whether Jesus withdrew primarily to get away from the crowd, or out of concern for what they would do or in preparation for walking on water, it is clear that he prioritised seeking his Father whatever the circumstances. We see that grief didn't stop him, as in Matthew 14 Jesus hears of the death of John the Baptist—his cousin—and withdraws privately to a solitary place. He went to be alone, to seek the comfort of God in his grief. I do find it quite remarkable that even in his grief, when the crowds catch up with him, "He had compassion on them and healed their sick."[122] Even in his grief and time with the Father being interrupted, he had compassion. I would have told them all to go away and give me some space. What a Saviour! We see in the Gospels examples from busyness to grief, from discernment to concern, that there was no time that wasn't a good time to be alone with His Father. He

---

[120] Holy Bible, Luke 6:12, New International Version®, NIV® Copyright ©1973, 1978, 1984, 2011 by Biblica

[121] Holy Bible, John 6:15, New International Version®, NIV® Copyright ©1973, 1978, 1984, 2011 by Biblica

[122] Holy Bible, Matthew 14:14, New International Version®, NIV® Copyright ©1973, 1978, 1984, 2011 by Biblica

fiercely prioritised and guarded his time with the Father. It was regular and went with every circumstance.

'Let us Go'

We now turn to an example described in Mark (It is also described in Luke) where I believe we see Jesus' fierce pursuit of the Father leading him during great need and great success to move on. In Mark 1:33–35 it says:

The whole town gathered at the door and Jesus healed many who had various diseases. He also drove out many demons, but he would not let the demons speak because they knew who he was. Very early in the morning, while it was still dark, Jesus got up, left the house and went off to a solitary place, where he prayed. Simon and his companions went to look for him and when they found him, they exclaimed: "Everyone is looking for you!" Jesus replied, "Let us go somewhere else – to the nearby villages – so I can preach there, also. That is why I have come."[123]

In a moment of apparent ministry success and great fruit, Jesus stops and spends time in prayer. Imagine, for a moment, the whole town gathered at the door. It must have been overwhelming, perhaps scary. The mob were all wanting their needs met and gathered clambering to get to the front and to be seen by this prophet. Jesus heals many and drives out many demons. This was a dramatic, powerful, life-changing evening. The text says

---

[123] Holy Bible, Mark 1:33–35, New International Version®, NIV® Copyright ©1973, 1978, 1984, 2011 by Biblica

they arrived after sunset, so who knows what time they all left and Jesus got to go to sleep! He must have been exhausted and, yet, even in this moment it says, "Very early in the morning, whilst it was still dark." Jesus knew in this moment of tiredness and high demand he needed to seek the Father. He needed his Father's wisdom and direction.

These moments of high demand and tiredness can often be the exact moment when we give ourselves permission to 'give it a miss'. We'll take time out with God when the busy period is over, when things have calmed down. We need some good sleep to be ready for the demands of the next day and yet it is in this moment Jesus knows the importance of taking the time to fiercely pursue time with his Father.

The first challenge for us is our willingness to pursue time with the Father during the busiest and potentially most fruitful moments. In fact, it is in these moments we must humble ourselves, recognising again that it is God who is doing it through us and the glory must go to Him. The second challenge, however, is that Jesus in this time with the Father knows something of his direction leading them on. This was a time of fruitful ministry, surely this was the time to stay where the people were teachable and much could be done for the sake of the Gospel. And yet when the disciples went looking, Jesus has a shocking announcement to make.

Imagine the disciples waking up after an incredible night of ministry, tired but buzzing from all they had witnessed —and suddenly, they realise Jesus isn't there. You can imagine people from the town had gone to gather friends, family members... anyone. Perhaps it was another knock on the door in the morning that woke the disciples up from their slumber. Whichever way it happened, Simon Peter and the others are pursued by more people, so much so, they exclaim, "Everyone is looking for you!"

"Everyone" is an interesting word to use as it suggests at least more than one or two. A crowd had formed again or, perhaps, it was just a handful, but the disciples were trying to hunt him down. Where has he gone? Why isn't he here? Doesn't he know they are all waiting for him? The disciples were caught up in the demands of ministry, in the awareness of the great need and opportunity in front of them. So much so that there is a sense of frustration, or even annoyance, that Jesus has chosen this moment to go off for a walk and pray. Jesus' response, however, fiercely combats the temptation to be led by need and not by God. There was a lesson for the disciples and also for us: don't let the need of others, the opportunity, the sense of fulfilment or transformation guide you. His response is simple: "Let us go somewhere else." He goes on to explain: "To the nearby villages, so I can preach there also." It is interesting that there doesn't seem to be a clear directive about where they are going. It doesn't seem that the Father has said to Jesus to go to a specific place but, rather, to leave where they currently are. This is more about communicating that it's time to move on rather than suggesting 'this is where you must go'.

This command "Let us Go" seems counterintuitive; surely this was the moment to stay. Was this command simply because Jesus was called to preach the Kingdom of God all around Israel; or was it also directly challenging the motives, the driver for ministry in the hearts of the disciples? Jesus lives, as we saw earlier, for the praise and recognition of the Father and does only what the Father is doing and, therefore, obeys and they move on. You can imagine the whispers from the disciples as they walk away from the town turning to one another saying, "What is He thinking?"; or "Surely, this can't be right." But Jesus fiercely shows them that it is all about obedience, not fame or success.

As we seek to walk in Jesus' way of fiercely pursuing time with the Father, what should this time look like?

Seeking encounter

Over the years I have come to recognise that's it not the form of what my time with God takes, the amount of time I spend reading the Bible or praying, but the intentional pursuit I have for encounter. That word "encounter" simply means "run into"[124] and running into God, bumping into him and having a conversation, is what we all need. If you run into a friend in town, you stop, catch up and you might even go and grab a coffee if you have time. You could have just sent them an email or a message on social media, but nothing beats actual face to face contact for building relationship.

I've often, over the years, spent time doing good things when spending time with God and, yet, not had a heart-to-heart with the God I was supposed to be seeking. It can easily become an academic exercise or a shopping

---

[124] https://www.vocabulary.com/dictionary/encounter#:~:text=Definitions%20of%20encounter,collect%20in%20one%20place

list prayer task, but afterwards, I recognised that I hadn't encountered God at all. I wasn't seeking His face, but I'd ended up seeking His hands for what he could give me rather than seeking His face for relationship with Him. I would like to encourage you, no matter how much time you have before you, to intentionally quieten yourself as you come before God to seek His face, listen and be still. Long before you dive into your petitions and prayer requests, seek to simply be in His presence. If, like me, you quickly rush on, pull yourself back and be still once again. I have often surprised myself with how often I've opened my Bible and not prayed before I've started reading. It was almost like I was ticking something off my to do list. Bible reading—tick! Simply Stopping for thirty-seconds and asking God to speak to me, to reveal himself to me more through His Word before I turn to it, helps me read it with encounter lenses on. I stop reading it like any other book and, instead, have my heart and my eyes attentive to what he wants to highlight to me.

I remember many years ago, a friend of mine told me that they were reading a verse of the Bible at a time and refused to move on from that verse until God had planted it in their hearts. They memorised and chewed up and digested this verse until they felt it was time to move on. I was challenged by this as I often get caught up in trying to read a whole chapter or section rather than really letting God's Word take root in my heart.

Time with God should be life-giving not life-guilting. We don't spend time with God because we have to but because we want to. Often, however, especially in my experience, if we are from a Christian background or in some form of leadership, we can carry a lot of guilt around this. The amount of time we spend with God (What is enough time?) and if we don't spend any time at all, the danger is we see ourselves as hypocrites who shouldn't be leading others at all.

As we think about Jesus' pursuit of time with the Father, we seek to be inspired by his example, not made guilty for what we fail to do for "there is now no condemnation for those who are in Christ Jesus".[125] I know I have often felt guilty for what I have or haven't done and have experienced that this sense of guilt stops me going back to God straight away but makes me continue to walk away from time with Him.

Over the years, I have beaten myself up for not being able to get up at five a.m. or six a.m. to spend hours with God. I wanted to do that and throughout my twenties and thirties, I would try and set my alarm early, but would often manage a single day and then be exhausted for the rest of the week, unable to get up at all until the last possible moment. I have now accepted that I am an owl! I am most awake in the evenings not the mornings and I accept that waking early is not something I can naturally do easily. Having said that, I find that spending time in the morning with God is important for me as I go into my day. So, I prioritise that but I also, in my current season, prioritise other moments in the day to connect with God. There are lots of biblical references to seeking God in the morning, not least the examples of Jesus we have looked at, but if evening is a better time for you then go for it. Perhaps a moment with God first thing in your day with

---

[125] Holy Bible, Romans 8:1, New International Version®, NIV® Copyright ©1973, 1978, 1984, 2011 by Biblica

time at the end to spend quality time is the right mix for you. Psalm 63:6–8 says, "When I remember you upon my bed and meditate on you in the watches of the night; for you have been my help and in the shadow of your wings I will sing for joy. My soul clings to you; your right hand upholds me."[126] If you are that night owl, feel released to go and spend time with God when you are most engaged.

A danger for me is that I can tick off that I have spent time with God and then get on with the rest of my day. I ignore God and do what I want instead of letting my time with God shape my awareness of Him throughout the whole day, leading to listening and conversation and journeying with Jesus all day long. I have also learned that seasons of life mean that routines need to change.

When our children were young, I used to feel guilty about my inability to spend a large chunk of time with God, until I accepted that, perhaps, it was an invitation to learn to be with Jesus all the time and grab moments of Bible reading and stillness where I could and be kind to myself during it. In his book 'Be Still' Brian Heasley helpfully describes, "In every season it is possible to find something that works. For Jesus the flow of his life and ministry was prayerful, reflective and overflowed from regular encounter with his Father."[127]

Whatever season you find yourself in, try to not evaluate it according to previous seasons but, instead, based on

---

[126] Holy Bible, Psalm 63:6–8, New International Version®, NIV® Copyright ©1973, 1978, 1984, 2011 by Biblica

[127] Brian Heasley, Be Still, SPCK, 2021, Pg 12

encountering God. It is so easy to see God as some strict evaluator rating us on the quality of our quiet time rather than a dad loving being with his kids whatever they have going on. 1 Chronicles 16:11 says, "Seek the Lord and his strength, seek his presence continually!"[128] This should be our aim, learning to seek God and His strength and his presence not just for the few minutes we have in the morning but all the time.

Joyce Huggett describes what changed when she had an encounter with God: "I could not stop myself praying. I prayed as I walked to the shops. I prayed as I met the children from school. I prayed when I went to bed and when I got up in the morning. But the nature of the prayer had changed. It ceased to be a string of requests, a tirade of questionings, beseechings and plaguings. Instead, the sense of the presence of God's life within stunned me into silence. This awed silence gave birth to wordless praise, wordless adoration and wordless consecration of my life to him."[129] This is a real life of prayer so much deeper, more profound, less religious and more transformative. It is important to remember, however, that, "The truth is that the origin of our desire for God is God's desire for us."[130] He wants to spend time with us; we don't have to persuade him to meet with us—He loves

---

[128] Holy Bible, 1 Chronicles 16:11, New International Version®, NIV® Copyright ©1973, 1978, 1984, 2011 by Biblica

[129] Joyce Huggett, Listening To God, Hodder & Stoughton, 1986

[130] Ruth Haley Barton, Invitation to Solitude and Silence, SPCK, 2021

it when we draw near to Him and he promises, 'draw near to God and He will draw near to you.'" (James 4:8).[131]

Seeking encounter not religious activity is what makes the difference, spiritual disciplines are helpful vehicles to take us towards the presence of God but on their own, they are simply just vehicles. It is the presence, the voice and the face of God that should be our primary aim. Francis Chan writes, "While others rush into prayer with opinions and demands, we cautiously approach His throne in reverence. Like the High priest entering the Holy of Holies, we treat prayer as sacred."[132] Sacred is not often something I'd describe my quiet time as being but, perhaps, considering it in this way might make it more a place of encounter rather than a job to get done.

Humbling self before God

Jesus modelled a life of pursuit of the Father but he also fiercely fought for and taught his disciples to do the same. In Matthew 6:5–6 Jesus says, "And when you pray, do not be like the hypocrites, for they love to pray standing in the synagogues and on the street corners to be seen by others. Truly I tell you, they have received their reward in full. But when you pray, go into your room, close the door and pray to your Father, who is unseen. Then your Father, who sees what is done in secret, will

---

[131] Holy Bible, James 4:8, New International Version®, NIV® Copyright ©1973, 1978, 1984, 2011 by Biblica

[132] Francis Chan, Letters to the Church, David C Cook, 2018, Pg 31

reward you."[133] Here, we see Jesus harshly rebuking those who pray to show off or for the crowd to see. Instead, Jesus encourages his followers to seek God in secret and in solitude. Jesus wanted his disciples to humble themselves before God and to prioritise doing this on their own. Does this mean we should never pray in front of others? Not at all; we see Jesus praying and singing with his disciples, but Jesus knows the importance of a real, honest and humble relationship with the Father that is fostered in the secret place. If Jesus modelled and taught for this in his followers, how do we fiercely fight for this in our teams where we are serving?

1. **Fiercely seeking solitude personally:** I can remember my team leader on my first youth work role getting us together for a team meeting and sending us off for half an hour to spend time with God before we returned to plan. After I had done this, my team leader commented that when I spend time with God, I was noticeably different when I returned. She commented that there was a tangible difference that I didn't necessarily notice myself. From this, I started running my own diary. I made a decision to clear Friday mornings as a space to retreat and pray and spend extended time with God. I appreciate it is a luxury, as I was able to get it agreed with those I was accountable to which many others might not be able to. I have kept this practice ever since. It is amazing how this time is contended for with different demands coming along to try and steal this time. I am not religious

---

[133] Holy Bible, Matthew 6:5–6, New International Version®, NIV® Copyright ©1973, 1978, 1984, 2011 by Biblica

about it but as much as possible keep nine a.m. to twelve p.m. clear to study, pray, journal, walk and worship.

At certain points, this has been a lifeline when daily rhythm has been rushed. At other times it has just been a moment to stop and reflect and give space for God to speak outside of all the meetings, calls and messages that fill my time. I have at points, had a monthly or half-termly retreat day instead of the weekly rhythm, depending on what was going on in my work. A whole day out can often be incredibly fruitful to completely stop and I'd recommend switching your phone off when you do this. Journalling can be helpful to reflect on different areas of your life, to express how you are feeling and what is filling your heart and your mind. Sometimes, painting or finding an artistic outlet can help express what is going on internally. Giving attention to your heart, your journey with God and your pursuit of the Father is so important. Exploring different ways to connect with God can be helpful rather than just remaining in our comfort zone or traditions. I have found contemplative prayer and the Northumbrian Community Prayer Book to be incredibly helpful, even though this is not something I had ever engaged in before. Jesus sought his Father regularly and if we are to follow in his way, we must do the same. Also, if we want to fiercely encourage our team to do the same, we must do it for ourselves because we shouldn't ask others to do what we aren't prepared to do ourselves.

2. **Permission giving and accountability:** As well as modelling by taking time out to seek God, we need

to set a culture of this being a priority for our team by giving permission for them to do the same. Often in an appraisal or reviewing how things are going with our team, we focus purely on the function of our team: how are we performing and delivering what we wanted to deliver? A way to fiercely protect and advocate for our team pursuing time with the Father is to ask how people are doing in terms of their relationship with Jesus and their walk with Him. It is important to say that this should not be used as some kind of power or manipulation or judgement from those leading but an opportunity to encourage and give space to team members to do this. A good way of doing this is to encourage all our team to have mentors or disciplers who are investing in their walk with Jesus outside of their leading. In SWYM, we place a high value on the place of mentoring, making it a key part of all courses that each trainee has a mentor in their local church placement setting who is purely focused on encouraging the individual in their personal and spiritual life outside of their responsibility and service. As a result of having a high priority for our trainees, we have added it as a requirement for all staff to also have someone they are accountable to who is helping them to continue to be growing and pursuing more of the God at work in their lives. At all our staff annual reviews there is a page which includes questions such as:

A. How is your walk with God?

B. How are things going with your mentor?

C. Can you share with us some recent answers to prayer?

We have found as we have added these questions annually that, sometimes, a mentor relationship needs to be reviewed or changed and some struggles or challenges are shared. This is then mentioned in regular line management. In all those I line manage, my first question before any other is simply: "How are you?" I linger on it to let people talk about what is going on with them. Sometimes, people might talk about their family and their walk with Jesus; simply giving them space to talk and then setting some goals around their development each time as well as the responsibilities/ tasks section is so important. I try and encourage members of our team to take time out to retreat, encouraging them to take some extended time out to seek God. This might have a discernment agenda if a big decision is looming or simply because life is a bit overwhelming at that moment. Moments to be still are so important.

Whatever our role and supervision of our teams, taking time out to ask how each team member is doing in their pursuit of the Father. It communicates that how people are doing in their relationship with God is more important than what they are achieving in their role. Having team members pursuing the Father will impact your whole team outlook, heart and focus but, also, the team members individually will feel valued and released. It's a win, win!

Jesus fiercely pursued time with the Father. He prioritised in every circumstance seeking solitude with his Father and calls us to walk in his way and to fiercely walk humbly with our God.

Pause | Selah

1. Take time to be holy, speak oft with thy Lord; Abide in Him always and feed on His Word. Make friends of God's children, help those who are weak, Forgetting in nothing His blessing to seek.

2. Take time to be holy, the world rushes on; Spend much time in secret, with Jesus alone. By looking to Jesus, like Him thou shalt be; Thy friends in thy conduct His likeness shall see.

3. Take time to be holy, let Him be thy Guide; And run not before Him, whatever betide. In joy or in sorrow, still follow the Lord and, looking to Jesus, still trust in His Word.

4. Take time to be holy, be calm in thy soul, Each thought and each motive beneath His control. Thus led by His Spirit to fountains of love, Thou soon shalt be fitted for service above.

William Longstaff[134]

---

[134] William Longstaff, Take Time to be Holy, The United Methodist Hymnal, No 395

Questions for reflection/discussion

1. How do you feel your personal pursuit of the Father is going right now? What might need to change? What more could you explore to find a freshness with this?

2. Do you have anyone who asks you personally about how your pursuit of the Father is going? If so, how honest are you being about this? If not, who could you ask to hold you to account?

3. As a team, how can you encourage and support one another to make your relationship with God a high priority and one that is spoken of when you get together?

4. What does it mean for you, as a team, as you serve to fiercely protect the pursuit of the Father with both your team and those you are trying to serve together?

> *The discipline of rest both helps others know that we are not always available but also reminds ourselves that life, work and ministry goes on just fine without us.*

Chapter 5
Fiercely Resting

"But the body must be weaned away from its tendencies to take control, to run the world, to achieve and produce, to attain gratification."
Dallas Willard[135]

"So then, there remains a Sabbath rest for the people of God, for whoever has entered God's rest has also rested from his works as God did from his."
Hebrews 4:9–10[136]

A few years ago, when my Grandma died, we were left a bit of money. As a part of this, we thought it might be good to spend some of it on a holiday of a lifetime, one of those experiences you would never forget and we would remember Gran whenever we thought of it. We decided to go to Northern Finland and to have a Lapland holiday. We found the perfect log cabin to stay in and planned out all the activities. As the time approached and the flights were booked, we started to get excited but then Covid-19 happened and we had to cancel two years in a row. Compared to what others went through it was nothing but we waited in the hope we might be able to go at some other point.

---

[135] Dallas Willard, Renovation of the Heart, SPCK, 2021, Pg 182

[136] Holy Bible, Hebrews 4:9–10, New International Version®, NIV® Copyright ©1973, 1978, 1984, 2011 by Biblica

Finally, the time came when we were able to rebook and make the holiday happen. Everything was booked and paid for, including husky dog rides and a hire car. We booked to stay the night before in a hotel by the airport as we had an early flight. The alarm went off at four-fifteen a.m. ready for us to get up and get to the airport. We arrived two hours before take-off and headed to drop our bags and get through security; however, the queues were like nothing I had seen before. Clearly, there were a huge number of flights leaving that morning.

We queued slowly to check the bags in and, eventually, that was done and we joined the security queue. We followed the queues back and forward on the way to the front. Eventually, we got to the front to discover that two of our bags needed to be checked-in but there were only two people working their way through a lot of bags. We started to get anxious as we were now only forty-five minutes from take-off. We waited patiently until we were called forward and then my phone pinged to say it was the last call for the flight. We tried to speed up the lady checking through our bags while she chatted away to her colleague. We had all our bags with twenty-five minutes until the flight set off. We walked around the corner to a sign saying that the boarding gates were a twenty-five-minute walk! We all panicked and just like in the movies, we ran—a family chasing through crowds down corridors, past shops. We ran and we ran!

Finally, we arrived at the gate ten minutes before the flight was due to take off to be told that the gate was closed. We were too late! My wife and I exchanged confused and anxious looks. We pleaded with them to let us through, but the answer was no. We suddenly realised we were about to lose our holiday of a lifetime; we would have to walk back through security, get our car and drive home and miss it all. Then a family with a girl in a wheelchair appeared explaining that security had also held them up because of the wheelchair. We felt, perhaps, there was a small chance they might do something for them. A man in a security jacket appeared and I overheard him say that it was going to be more hassle to get the bags in the hold off the flight than to let us go on. The checkout lady stormed off, clearly wanting to hold fast to the rules; but with huge amounts of thank yous and relief they let us on the plane. We have often had battles to go on holiday whether illness, accident or things falling through, but this was another level. As we sat on the plane, adrenaline poured through our bodies as we realised just how close we had come to losing it all and how grateful we were to be sitting on the plane.

We had to fight for our holiday—we had to fight to rest. Making time to prioritise rest is a battle. It isn't something that just happens, it is a choice and something for which we must contend. God rested on the seventh day not because he'd completed his to-do list and couldn't think of anything else to do, He rested as a choice He created and worked and then He consciously stopped to rest. John Mark Comer wrote, "The word *rested* in Genesis 2 is 'shabat' in Hebrew, where we get the word Sabbath. It essentially means 'to stop' or 'cease' or 'be complete' but it can also be translated 'to celebrate'. We have to cease, to stop, to celebrate and this requires a conscious decision." [137]

---

[137] John Mark Comer, Garden City, Zondervan, 2017

Come Away

Jesus modelled rest and celebration. Even though the Gospels take us through the highs and lows of Jesus' life and ministry, you still get a window into his rhythm of sabbath and rest. I would love to have been able to sit with the disciples eating, laughing and resting together after a busy period of ministry. What a privilege to rest with him and yet an invitation he still gives to us today to do the same. In Mark 6:31, we read: "And he said to them, 'Come away by yourselves to a desolate place and rest a while.' For many were coming and going and they had no leisure even to eat."[138]

Jesus understood what it was to be busy and, therefore, understood the importance of rest. Coffman comments, "Mark alone notes no less than eleven occasions on which Jesus retired from his work."[139] This was a priority for Jesus. It is easy to forget that Christ was there at Creation; in fact, "by him all things were made"[140] and he was also there on the seventh day resting with the Father and the Spirit. He has always rested and, therefore, he maintained this rhythm. Barkley adds, "Here we see what might be called the rhythm of the Christian life. The Christian life is a continuous going into the presence of God from the presence of men and coming out into the

---

[138] Holy Bible, Mark 6:31, New International Version®, NIV® Copyright ©1973, 1978, 1984, 2011 by Biblica

[139] James Coffman, Commentary on Mark, Firm Foundation Publishing House, 1975

[140] Holy Bible, Colossians 1:16, New International Version®, NIV® Copyright ©1973, 1978, 1984, 2011 by Biblica

presence of men from the presence of God. It is like the rhythm of sleep and work. We cannot work unless we have our time of rest."[141]

Jesus' invitation to come away is for everyone, it's an invitation to stop and to recreate. It is an invitation to be renewed, to feast, to celebrate, to worship. I don't know about you, but I can often use my rest time badly, doing things that don't restore me. Getting out in creation, making or doing something creative, having a nice meal, spending time with family and friends is renewing for me. These things help me to stop working and thinking about work and to be refreshed. Ruth Haley Barton comments on this: "There is an energy that comes from being rested that is different from the energy that comes from being driven. There is a wisdom that comes from silent listening that is different from what comes from talking things to death. There is right action that comes from waiting on God that is utterly different from reactivity."[142] Rest gives space for God to speak, for us to have space to listen and to pause.

I find it interesting that Jesus takes them away to a "desolate place"; a place away from the crowd. I am a huge fan of the outdoors, so I need to be aware that, for some, this isn't how they best rest. But for me, there is something here about isolation, away from demands and the pressing needs of others that helps us to rest.

---

[141] William Barclay, Gospel of Mark, St Andrew Press, 1975

[142] Ruth Haley Barton, Invitation to Solitude and Silence, SPCK, 2021

Workaholic?

I know I have the potential to be a workaholic. I have a brilliant wife who has always been really good at holding me to account about stopping. I know that if she didn't, I could just keep going and going because the work is never done. There is a danger in our culture and society that we celebrate workaholic tendencies, which I find disturbing. We celebrate busyness as if busyness means success. We expect people to reply to messages instantly and be available when we need them and find it frustrating when they are not.

A few years ago, I made a conscious decision to never say, "I'm really busy" when asked how I was. I just found everywhere I went I and others would give this as a reply. In the end, I felt challenged that I cannot complain about being too busy constantly and not change my behaviour. I knew I was looking for some kind of validation or recognition for my busyness, whether it was respect, sympathy or something else. There was more going on internally than just saying I was busy. I've realised that by saying these words I was giving others the impression I didn't have time for them, or that they would be adding to my busyness. I've found people more open with me through not saying these words.

However, just saying we aren't busy and still being so busy that we can't stop is not the answer. We need to change our behaviour and our words. I certainly have experienced moments where I have been so busy with a run of events, evenings, weekends etc., where I have felt on the edge, not healthy or safe. This should not be the norm for any leader. We must learn to walk a balanced, rested life. The truth is that we can and must rest. If we cannot stop, we are inadvertently communicating that everything depends on us. "I can't stop, too much to do." "I can't stop, or this won't happen." The world will keep spinning and in fact things will go on just fine without us, it is arrogance and pride to think otherwise. Fierce Humility means to fight to make ourselves stop. To fight for rest when the world is pressing in. To stop even when we think we can't.

In my experience of working with leaders, it's often not a conscious decision to burn out. They didn't decide to do eighty or one-hundred-hour weeks over and over. It just gradually happened. They added a new course, activity, outreach project and before they knew it, they had no space. Often, it is the result of bad planning. We didn't put any toil time in the diary to replace the day off we had to work through. Often when we are busy, it is hard to look ahead in the diary to do this, but a wise friend of mine once said, "Are you running your diary or is your diary running you." John Mark Comer helpfully writes, "The solution to an over busy life is not more time. It is to slow down and simplify our lives around what really matters."[143]

If you are reading this and are feeling overwhelmed and this feeling is more than just a busy moment but has been going on for too long and become your norm, be ruthless. Go to those you are accountable to and work out what needs to change. What can be cut out of your schedule or responsibilities? What can be delegated to others? The truth is that busyness stops our availability to God and to others. If we are busy, in my experience, our personal time with God suffers. We are so busy desperately trying

---

[143] John Mark Comer, Ruthless Elimination of Hurry, John Murray Press, 2019

to achieve that we miss the relational journey of adventure and trust and dependence on God. We also make ourselves unavailable to others. Henri Neuwen wrote, "When our souls are restless, when we are driven by thousands of different and often conflicting stimuli, when we are always 'over there' between people, ideas and the worries of this world, how can we possibly create the room and space where someone else can enter freely without feeling himself an unlawful intruder?"[144] If I need help, I'm not going to ask the person who is stressed, tired and communicating "don't disturb me" with their body language.

Not only might we make ourselves unavailable, but we can get to a stage where we see people as those we can use rather than those we can serve. We become so focused on tasks and projects and our needs that we don't listen or prefer or honour those in front of us. Neuwen continues, "So we find it extremely hard to pay attention because of our intentions, as soon as our intentions take over, the question no longer is, 'Who is he? But 'What can I get from him?'—and then we no longer listen to what he is saying but to what we can do with what he is saying."[145] This is deeply challenging for people like me. I must be rested so that I might be disciplined to not let this behaviour start to happen in my life.

Often, those of us who have a tendency towards being a workaholic need to return to the first chapter of this book.

---

[144] Henri Nouwen, Wounded Healer, Darton, Longman & Todd Ltd, 2014

[145] Henri Nouwen, Wounded Healer, Darton, Longman & Todd Ltd, 2014

Finding your security and identity in God and not in your work or service. When you see yourself in the way God sees us and don't seek to prove yourself to others through a pursuit of success or respect, then you will find it much easier to rest, to sabbath weekly, to stop. Stopping releases you and others. We just need to practice stopping. It reminds me of when learning to drive: sometimes it has to be an emergency stop to make sure we don't hurt ourselves or others, but it's much less traumatic if we just learn to break regularly. It makes the journey far smoother and less stress-inducing. Dallas Willard writes, "But the body must be weaned away from its tendencies to take control, to run the world, to achieve and produce, to attain gratification."[146] This is a critical issue for leaders today.

Often, we don't want to stop because we either think we are indispensable or, if we are honest, we quite like being needed. The discipline of rest both helps others know that we are not always available but also reminds ourselves that life, work and ministry goes on just fine without us. Jen Wilkins makes this point very clearly: "Our patterns of work and rest reveal what we believe to be true about God and ourselves. God alone requires no limits on his activity. To rest is to acknowledge that we humans are limited by design. We are created for rest just as surely as we are created for labor. An inability or unwillingness to cease from our labours is a confession of unbelief, an admission that we view ourselves as creator and sustainer of our own universes."[147] We simply need to STOP!

---

[146] Dallas Willard, Revolution of Character, Navpress, 2005, Pg 141

[147] Jen Wilkin, Ten words to live by, Crossway, 2021

Not pharisaic but disciplined

I have, over the years, read many books around the discipline of sabbath. I am always challenged as someone who has a strong work ethic and enjoys being busy. One thing I have always been challenged by has been the call to totally cease anything that takes effort, rather than ceasing from work. I know friends who grew up in families where Sabbath was observed and there was to be no TV and no cinema on these days as they should be kept Holy for the Lord. I both respect and struggle with this.

The Pharisees, in Jesus' day, seemed to take the commandments and add a whole raft of extra rules to outwork the commandment. This created a law that was like a chain around the necks of the Jews. Jesus, when challenged about his disciples picking some heads of grain and eating them on the Sabbath, was asked, "Look! Your disciples are doing what is unlawful on the Sabbath."[148] Jesus replies by referring back to David and the Son of Man before they try and catch Jesus out when they see a man with a shrived hand and they ask, "Is it lawful to heal on the Sabbath?"[149] Instead of being in awe that this man could be healed and valued and restored, they wanted to trick this Rabbi into breaking their own rules. Jesus' reply is brilliant: "If any of you has a sheep and falls into a pit on the Sabbath, will you not take hold

---

[148] Holy Bible, Matthew 12 v 2, New International Version®, NIV® Copyright ©1973, 1978, 1984, 2011 by Biblica

[149] Holy Bible, Matthew 12 v 10, New International Version®, NIV® Copyright ©1973, 1978, 1984, 2011 by Biblica

of it and lift it out? How much more valuable is a person than a sheep! Therefore, it is lawful to do good on the Sabbath."[150]

Jesus seems to find a grace and a pragmatism around the Sabbath rather than a restrictive, guilt-ridden law that the Pharisees had. Sabbath is for ceasing work, for worship and celebration, but does that mean we don't help someone in need? This is where we must not become Pharisaical, looking to revel in our law keeping and dishonouring others in the process. If I choose to not do anything on the Sabbath, does that mean making my wife a cup of tea, walking the dog, putting a load of washing on are forbidden?

Jesus, of course, helpfully added: "The Sabbath was made for man, not man for the Sabbath."[151]

God has given us the Sabbath for our good to be a blessing to us not because He is testing us or because it is a burden. He knows it is good for our well-being to stop, to worship, to rest and to refuel.

Don't get me wrong, we can easily use this as an excuse to keep on working or to not try and keep our work, our chores restricted to the other six days in the week. As busy twenty-first century people, it is much more likely that we will not stop rather than being Pharisaical over our Sabbath so we must learn to stop. If I say to the

---

[150] Holy Bible, Matthew 12 v 11- 12, New International Version®, NIV® Copyright ©1973, 1978, 1984, 2011 by Biblica

[151] Holy Bible, Mark 2 v 27, New International Version®, NIV® Copyright ©1973, 1978, 1984, 2011 by Biblica

farmer, you must not work on the Sabbath, does he make the cows and sheep fast for the day? Of course not! However, doing a minimum amount on one day and finding time for worship and rest is surely the wise way to go. This requires discipline to plan and order our weeks so we can stop because we know it is good for us. We want to worship, stop and refuel but not because it is legalism tying us up in knots. Shelly Miller helpfully said, "Sabbath isn't about resting perfectly; it's about resting in the One who is perfect."[152] This is helpful to order things in our minds. Dallas Willard adds that, "Sabbath is inseparable from worship and, indeed, genuine worship is Sabbath."[153] This is helpful as it helps us see that being proud in our ceasing isn't actually Sabbath if it isn't an offering of worship.

The danger is that you have a busy weekend of activities and go into your week overwhelmed, tired and stressed instead of rested. When you do this, you can make it worse by adding guilt on top that you haven't truly stopped. These are the moments to receive the grace of God and to plan differently next time so that we are genuinely renewed. This whole area of rest, in my experience, is a life's work so don't beat yourself up, run back to the Father and learn how best you rest.

As we seek to model rest well as leaders, we must also fiercely fight for it in our teams. So, what might this look like practically.

---

[152] Shelly Miller, Rhythms of Rest, Baker, 2016

[153] Dallas Willard, The Great Omission, Monarch Books, 2006

1. Fiercely protecting those on your team by encouraging rest

What we choose to do influences others. We reproduce after kind and so if we model an unhealthy work/life balance we are suggesting in our behaviour that we expect the same in our team. We need to learn to rest well for the sake of our own soul and for our families and the health of our ministry for the long term but also for the health of our team and the culture of our team.

I've noticed, over the years, that if I'm not taking holiday or time back in lieu, then I am far less likely to be strict with my team that they do the same. In line management or team contexts, choosing to not celebrate busyness but celebrate good balance can be really helpful. Every time I sit down with my team, I ask them how they are doing and set aside a specific moment to ask if they have booked holiday and time off in lieu. I was recently at a conference where the speaker shared how busy they had been and their crazy last few days of frantic ministry leading up to this current point. I was disturbed as I looked around and saw people either applauding or admiring this way. I was shocked as I saw unhealthy boundaries and overwork celebrated so publicly. I believe Jesus would have fiercely criticised this kind of behaviour and I wonder if in our 24/7 Western culture, we have allowed our culture to invade the Church, rather than the peace and rest of God invading the world through the Church. We celebrate busyness by praising those doing too much and being critical of those who say, "No" when asked to do something outside of their current commitments.

We also need to be careful that we are not adding more and more jobs, events and activities to our team without removing things from the list at the same time. Adding more is unsustainable unless you have the resources of more volunteers or staff to help make those things happen. Modelling and encouraging rest can look like pruning back work and taking things from people rather than simply adding more all the time and expecting people to not be overwhelmed and overworked.

Encouraging and sharing stories of those resting and resting well is important and explaining our behaviour is important, too. As a result of the stage of life I am currently in I need a couple of days a week to collect my children from school, meaning I finish work earlier than normal. I then catch up with a little work in the evening. The challenge is that people assume I don't stop work, sending emails at eight p.m. or nine p.m. I explain to my team what happens with me so they don't think I expect them to work until nine o'clock in the evening. I also seek to try and challenge friends and colleagues if they send emails or messages at inappropriate times of the day or night. Don't get me wrong, I am far from perfect; WhatsApp can be particularly hard to get away from and some of my team would say I regularly slip up in keeping tight boundaries, but I am determined to model a healthy team culture around rest and days off. I'd encourage you to do the same, not with a judging harsh criticism, but with gracious encouragement.

2. Encouraging thankfulness

Michael Ramsey said that "Thankfulness is a soil in which pride does not easily grow."[154] Encouraging a culture of thankfulness within our team will encourage appreciation for all that we have been given. Thankfulness helps us to stop and take stock.

I often find that workaholics and those that can't stop, do not find it easy to be thankful. Thankfulness requires stopping to appreciate, stopping to reflect and to be grateful. Sabbath rest creates space for thankfulness to grow. Bonhoeffer wrote, "It's very easy to overestimate the importance of our own achievements in comparison with what we owe to others."[155] Once again, there is a link between rest and thankfulness that we need to encourage in our teams. If we create a culture where we are thankful for all God has given us including our time, our families, our homes and rest we are more likely to look for opportunities to reflect and be thankful.

CJ Mahaney writes, "An ungrateful person is a proud person. If I'm ungrateful, I'm arrogant. And if I'm arrogant, I need to remember God doesn't sympathise with me in that arrogance He is opposed to the proud."[156] Rest helps thankfulness to grow, thankfulness helps worship to grow and worship helps humility to grow.

---

[154] David Brooks, The Road to Character , Penguin Books, 2016

[155] Dietrich Bonhoeffer, Letters and Papers from Prison, SCM Press, 2017

[156] C.J.Mahaney, Humility - True Greatness, Soverign Grace Ministries, 2005, Pg 71

If you want a culture in your team where you rest well, then making space to be thankful as a team will encourage a culture of reflection and rest where we recognise it is not us building whatever we are building, but God alone.

Before we move on to explore what it means to walk in fierce humility in front of others, let's take some time to pause and reflect on this topic, and how it is about acknowledging our own humanity and choosing to walk in fierce humility before God.

FIERCE HUMILITY

Pause | Selah

"Almost everything will work if you unplug it for a few minutes—including you."[157] Anne Lamott

---

[157] Anne Lamott, https://www.goodreads.com/quotes/6830146-almost-everything-will-work-again-if-you-unplug-it-for

Questions for reflection/discussion

1. What are your rhythms of rest like currently? What changes might you need to make to discover a healthier rhythm?

2. Do you struggle to stop and switch off? Do you have workaholic tendencies? Why do you think this might be?

3. What is your team culture like around rest? Do you celebrate busyness or healthy balance?

4. What habits of thankfulness could you build into your routines to help you to practice gratefulness?

> *It's perhaps, then, not really about releasing control but choosing to not try to take control.*

Chapter 6
Fiercely Releasing Not Controlling

"When the greatest leaders have done their work, the people say, 'We did it ourselves.'"[158]

Stephen Cottrell

"Let my people go."
Exodus 5:1[159]

It was an early morning meeting at a coffee shop just off the motorway with a local church leader. After having got our drinks, I sat and asked how things were going. As I listened, I didn't quite know what to do with myself. Here I was sitting listening to a mature leader who was clearly upset/frustrated that a member of their staff team was moving on. They explained to me the context, the reasoning behind the decision and the frustration at not knowing how or when they might fill the gap left behind. The leader was clearly in shock not having seen this decision coming and had clearly spent some time trying to persuade this person to reconsider. I understood the frustration and the minor panic, I've been there! It's not a nice feeling. The problem was that I couldn't quite believe

---

[158] Stephen Cottrell, Hit the Ground Kneeling, Church House Publishing, 2008, Pg 14

[159] Holy Bible, Exodus 5:1, New International Version®, NIV® Copyright ©1973, 1978, 1984, 2011 by Biblica

that this leader had reached this stage in their leadership journey and had not learned the lesson yet, that the leader's job is to release and hold people lightly, rather than trying to control them.

A friend of mine once used the fist example to help demonstrate what is going on in these moments. Whilst reading this let me invite you to make a fist with your hand and grip as tightly as you possibly can. Squeeze and keep squeezing until you can feel it hurting and straining, then hold that for a few seconds until it feels very uncomfortable. This is what it is like when we seek to hold on tightly to someone or something. Everything tenses, is strained and uncomfortable. As we grip on and try to stop anything getting out of our hands the stress builds. Now let go and open up your hand just holding it palm up, open. We feel a release of tension, an openness and freedom. This is what we are meant to do, to hold people, things in our life open-handedly. People may be currently placed into our hands for us to hold lightly but if we hold them lightly, God may well take them and move them on. But if He does, He will provide someone or something else. It is not our job to hold on tightly to others but to release people and things to God.

I expect you have heard someone say; "No! You don't do it like that, you NEED to do it like this." It may well have been followed by someone trying to grab our computer or phone to show us how it should be done. These are the kinds of words that come out of our mouths when we want something done how we would do it. This is control, which can be defined as "to try and influence or direct people's behaviour."[160]

Control freak?

The reason we try to control people or things is that we hate the feeling of being "out of control". We feel vulnerable, dangerous even. Instead of recognising this "out of control" feeling as an opportunity we, instead, choose to quickly grab hold of what we can control and hold on tightly. I'm sure if I ask you to think back over your life to some controlling leaders, it wouldn't take you very long. That leader who always had to have the last say or who had already made the decision before the meeting and simply had to convince everyone they were right. Simon Walker wrote, "Control offers us a sense of security—but it is perhaps wise to recognise that it is really only an illusion of security."[161] Control can be a self-defence mechanism but, of course, life cannot be controlled, there are always external influences, opinions, interruptions beyond our control. Walker goes on to say, "In an environment of fear, control is everything."[162] This would seem to suggest that it might even be a part of the fight or flight mechanism that when we are under threat, we fight by taking control. It is what helps us to feel safer.

Perhaps, like me, you know you have the potential to control situations, decisions or even people under your

---

[160] https://languages.oup.com/google-dictionary-en/

[161] Simon Walker, Leading out of who you are, Piquant Editions, 2007

[162] Simon Walker, Leading out of who you are, Piquant Editions, 2007

care. A few years ago, someone helpfully pointed out that if I was in a room people would defer to me. I can be a strong character, loud and opinionated and so when others highlighted this, it made me change my behaviour. For a while, I tried to fight it. I would desperately try not to jump into group discussions when I felt it was heading away from what I thought should happen. However, I soon learnt this was like trying to tell a dog not to chase a cat. What I needed to learn to do was to not be in the room. If I wasn't in the room, I could release others to have the conversation and make the decision without me having to shape it. There were meetings and discussions I had to be a part of; however, there were also a lot when I didn't, but I enjoyed the topic and wanted to have my say. It's not a nice thing to admit to having the potential to control others or things, but admitting is the beginning of being able to let go of control.

Controlling leaders often come across as power hungry, obsessive and insecure. Controlling leaders cannot let go and, ultimately, if they are unable to address their controlling behaviour they will leave a trail of disillusioned followers. These followers will feel they have been "used" and will feel that their potential has been capped. Controlling leaders can use people to achieve their ends and, just like my story at the start of the chapter, when people choose to leave or make decisions against them, the controlling leader will (having lost control) get angry, dismissive or stamp their authority to change their choice or decision. The term "control freak" is one that can easily be used for any of us who have a tendency to control and although this term itself is a negative one it is perhaps more normal than freakish in our society to control than to release.

Jesus once again is our teacher and our guide in all of this. His ministry was one of releasing others not seeking to control his reputation, his followers or even religious leaders. He sought to influence, to guide but not to control. Stepping back further for a moment, we should consider the "Missio Dei" (The Mission of God) as one of sending and releasing. God doesn't seek to control but in love sends. He sent His Son into the world, He sent his Spirit to the church, He sends us out into the world. It is part of the character of God to release, to let go of control. The fact that we have free will is a choice by our Creator to not control us but to release us to choose. We could have been robots forced to do His bidding, but we are his children released to choose to love and to walk away if we want to. Richard Rohr takes this further by adding, "We like control; God, it seems, loves vulnerability. In fact, if Jesus is the image of God, then God is much better described as 'Absolute Vulnerability Between Three' than 'All-mighty One'. Yet how many Christian prayers begin with some form of 'Almighty God'? If you're immersed in the Trinitarian mystery, you must equally say, 'All-Vulnerable God' too!"[163] We see here something of the opposite of control in the character of God. A fiercely humble vulnerability that releases others rather than seeking to control.

Two great examples of Jesus releasing include the rich young ruler and the sending out of the disciples. How was the rich young ruler released, you might ask? I find this interaction with Jesus deeply challenging. We find it in both Matthew and Mark as a man approaches Jesus seeking an answer from this Rabbi about eternal life. After

---

[163] Richard Rohr, The Divine Dance, SPCK, 2016

receiving an answer about the commandments, he asks, "What do I still lack?"[164] Jesus seems to mention what is first place in this man's heart: his wealth and possessions. He says, "If you want to be perfect, go, sell your possessions and give to the poor and you will have treasure in heaven. Then come, follow me." It is a hard call, a deeply challenging request. And what does the man do? "When the young man heard this, he went away sad, because he had great wealth."

We often reflect on the sadness of the man walking away, not able to give his all to follow Jesus, yet I'm confronted by the fact that Jesus allowed him to walk away. He didn't chase after him and ask him to re-consider, he didn't make the call less challenging. He didn't try to persuade him, he seemed to simply let him go, allowing him to make his decision and live with it. Wow! This goes against a lot of how I've seen the church in the West do mission. We soften the call of Jesus to get people to follow us, we make it as easy as possible, remove as many barriers and perhaps as a result we end up with half-hearted followers who only came because they were promised the earth when, in fact, the earth was what they were called to give up. Jesus did not try to control the situation or the decision, he stood back and watched as the man walked away. I'm sure the text could have said, "And Jesus watched him walk away and was also deeply sad."

Jesus sending out the disciples was also an act of releasing, giving control to the disciples. Even more so, ascending to heaven to leave the mission of the church

---

[164] Holy Bible, Matthew 19:16–22, New International Version®, NIV® Copyright ©1973, 1978, 1984, 2011 by Biblica

to this small band of followers was releasing, not controlling. If I was Jesus, I would perhaps have overseen a decade or two of mass revival and across continent mission before ascending, just to make sure the Gospel would definitely make it to every tribe and nation. But he goes and sends his Spirit to fill and enable them to do it in his name. Jesus, in Matthew 10, gathers the twelve and gives "them authority to drive out impure spirits and to heal every disease and sickness."[165] He has allowed them to see him do this for themselves; he has coached them and now he releases them and invites them to come back and reflect on what they have seen and done. This is a releasing leader, one who does not have to always be present to overrule or control their team. Parkinson comments, "More than any other biblical leader, it seems that, from the very outset of his ministry, Jesus is sharply focused on multiplying his own ministry through the empowering of others."[166]

The life God has called us to live is a life of dying to control through Jesus. Dying to our need to run our own lives. It's a radical call. A scary call at times. If we want to be leaders who last, we must learn to not control. Henri Nouwen helpfully wrote, "Here we touch the most important quality of Christian leadership in the future. It is not a leadership of power and control, but a leadership of powerlessness in which the suffering servant of God,

---

[165] Holy Bible, Matthew 10:1, New International Version®, NIV® Copyright ©1973, 1978, 1984, 2011 by Biblica

[166] Ian Parkinson, Understanding Christian Leadership, SCM Publishing, 2020, Pg 80

Jesus Christ is made manifest."[167] This picture of leadership goes against so much of western thought but a leadership of powerlessness, a leadership which releases control reveals the way and the person of Jesus.

Releasing

The definition of release is to "allow something to move, to act or to flow freely."[168] Releasing is letting go and stepping back and allowing things to grow and evolve without our dominance.

We have seen that the Godhead is releasing and that Jesus, as the image of the invisible God, modelled a releasing ministry. Often it is a challenge to not completely remove yourself altogether. If you do this, then the leader releases without support, reflection and wise counsel. Jesus seems to regularly have time with just the disciples for teaching and reflection whether on the meaning of his parables or on what had just happened (for example after the rich young ruler encounter). The kind of "releasing leader" who is never present when their team members are serving and leaves their team with no support or reflection, is disempowering their team in a significant way to the "controlling leader". I've often seen this when a leader wants something off their plate—perhaps a children's worker or a buildings manager or a community project—and once they are in place they release control completely, leaving the new

---

[167] Henri Nouwen, Wounded Healer, Darton, Longman & Todd Ltd, 2014

[168] Oxford Languages, https://languages.oup.com/google-dictionary-en/

person or project completely in the deep end with no encouragement or investment at all. This is not releasing but discarding. Releasing is proactive sending whilst not removing care and support. Parkinson writes, "Taking up legitimate power as a leader is very different from using it abusively. Not to take up properly designated power may itself be a denial of responsibility and may result in more harmful consequences for those for whom we should have a concern."[169]

Some questions to consider then are: Do we really look to release people into their gifts or seek to show off our own? Do we like to tell everyone what we are doing, have done or praise others with no mention of ourselves? Do we look to give away responsibility or are we afraid of what might happen if we do? What if they do it wrong? What if the church doesn't like it? What if God can't raise up this next generation because I'm standing in the way? What if God can't release others to lead because I don't trust them and my name is on the line?

Don't get me wrong, I'm not saying we don't take responsibility and do what we are asked to do and do the best that we can. There is a difference between not taking control and being irresponsible. I'm not advocating irresponsible behaviour; instead, I want to challenge where we like to be in control of things and to enable us to stop trying to control. If I say I release people but I don't, it would be better for me never to have said it because you end up with people feeling disempowered, unappreciated and their growth stunted.

---

[169] Ian Parkinson, Understanding Christian Leadership, SCM Publishing, 2020, Pg 116

You cannot control your reputation; you may think you can, but you can't. If you are seeking to follow Christ and seek first his Kingdom, you will be accused of all sorts. You may also find people who don't like you—but you cannot and will not be loved by everyone. Sorry to crush any illusions there! There will be people out there who think Paul does a great job at running SWYM, but others who think I have let them down and don't want to see me again. There will be people in your church who think you are the best thing since sliced bread, but there will be people who don't understand you. Don't pay too much attention to what people think. Pay attention to your heart. Are you jealous, angry at others, are you always trying to justify your actions, defend your corner? Are you on a one man/woman mission to get everyone to like you and think you are the best leader they have ever had in your church/project? We need to stop trying to control our reputation and recognition.

As we lead, we should be simply doing this for God as an offering. If God raises us up, he raises us up, if he lowers us down, he lowers us down. Look at Joseph: everyone thought he'd slept with Potiphar's wife and he ended up in prison. He was up-down-up-down in terms of reputation, but he allowed God to change his heart and to be obedient. We are called to serve faithfully wherever God places us. The challenge is that we want to short-cut to the good times. To rush to the vision, the prophetic picture or the job we want, ignoring the journey God wants to take us on that enables us to be the person he wants us to be in the setting he has called us to. We need to stop trying to control our future and ambition. Instead, focus on being obedient in the small things and leave the rest with Him. How freeing and liberating to not have to try to make it happen ourselves but to trust it with God.

This doesn't mean that we don't ever make decisions, with an attitude, "God will do it all, so I'll sit back". We must be faithful in what we have now. As I've grown older, I've come to realise that God cares much less about where we are and what we are doing and cares more about our heart wherever we are. We need to place ourselves in the place of releasing and trusting, not the place of controlling and taking hold of things before their time. When you need to make decisions about your future, don't look for pay packets and prestige, look for where you are going to be formed... grow in God the most. Are you trying to take short-cuts to what God has called you to or even to the things YOU want?

The truth is that it is impossible to control your life. You cannot do it. So, this idea of releasing control is a joke, we never had control. Trying to control your future, your reputation, your pain is impossible. If I told you to control a pack of playing cards and then threw them at you, you'd be left with perhaps one or two in your hands and a pile of cards all over the floor. It's an impossible task. It's perhaps, then, not really about releasing control but choosing to not try to take control. At the end of the day, trying to take control is a waste of energy, effort and time. Instead, follow your Master's way and be fiercely humble as you look to release others. So how do you practically go about releasing others in your team? What practical steps can you take to create a releasing culture?

1. Release responsibility not just tasks

A frequent mistake is to think you are releasing others when all you are doing is delegating tasks. Delegating continues to keep you in control of the end result and continues to give you the ability to dictate the direction of travel. Releasing responsibility gives away control. You might set the direction of travel but not say how to get there, releasing your team member to work out and be responsible for the how.

You might say, "Here is a project I'd love you to head up. Here is the planned goal but it is over to you to work out how to get there. If you get stuck or have any questions, I'm available so come back to me and I'll gladly help but I release you to plan, form team and work towards a common goal." This is very different from a delegator's approach which says, "We are running this event please can you book the venue, ring the PA company and book the equipment. Here is a list of what we need and send me a first draft of publicity for me to check and change." The difference is huge between these two approaches. In my experience, it is often busyness that makes us micro-manage when releasing and delegating responsibility frees up more time. But if you are feeling overwhelmed, you are more likely to try to control things around you so you don't get any nasty surprises.

Spread decision making wider

The wisdom of Jethro still rings true to the control freak. As Moses controlled judgements for the people and created a bottleneck, Jethro was able to look and see that delegating and widening decision making would solve a whole host of problems. Within your team, do you make all the decisions, or do you have to be present when decisions are made to oversee them? Look to spread decision making beyond, even beyond your core team. Doing so will release a wider pool of leaders but also makes you more effective. This will also mean that not only do you become a releasing leader, but you also encourage your team to release others as well. This will help create a releasing culture throughout your church/organisation that should last long before you have gone. Rowlands defines empowerment as "bringing people outside the decision-making process into it".[170] Who could you be bringing into the decision-making process on your team or around your team?

Let my people go

The famous call to Pharoah from God "Let my people go" is apt. Pharoah was not only controlling but enslaving and abusing the people of Israel. The call to controlling leaders is the same: "Let my people go." Jonathan Lamb states: "Leaders do not say, 'here I am,' but, 'there you are'. Their work is for

---

[170] Jo Rowlands, Empowerment Examined, Taylor and Francis, 1995

the benefit of others."[171] Jim Collins continues this theme: "A leader with a humble heart looks out the window to find and applaud the true causes of success and in the mirror to find and accept responsibility for failure."[172] This is a challenging thought: that you look to release and benefit others and applaud the success of others and stand back to accept where things have gone wrong and take responsibility, shielding your team from the flack. Returning to the opening example of the leader outraged at the departing of his staff member, I have made a decision that when a team member comes to me to say that they have decided to move on I graciously accept their decision. I will not challenge or persuade them and will do my absolute best to enable them to finish really well, ultimately releasing them to go with our blessing and thanks. This is not always easy to do and all parties must help make this happen.

I can remember years ago a leader saying to me that you are remembered more for how you left than all you achieved. I want to be someone who leaves well and enables others to leave well. If we are releasing leaders, we should expect to see people growing up and through our teams and moving on. If you are not, you should be asking, "Why?" You should aim to see up-and-coming leaders grow, learning from your mistakes. On the flip side, if you are seeing an incredibly high

---

[171] Jonathan Lamb, Leading with God Watching, IVP, 2006

[172] James Collins, Good to Great, Harper Collins Publishers Inc, 2001

turnover on your teams, you should be checking that you are not controlling or unsupportive and driving people out. Parkinson helpfully adds, "Our goal in growing and equipping others must never be to raise up people who will either always remain within our shadow or continue to be dependent in some way upon us. A good parent does not have children for them to remain as infants but rather works to prepare them for independent and fruitful adulthood. Our aspirations as leaders must always be to grow others who will not only thrive without us but, hopefully, in all ways outstrip us in effectiveness."[173]

Having looked at how Jesus fiercely released rather than controlled people, let's, before we move on to Jesus fierce vulnerability and accountability, stop to reflect on where we may need to change our thinking and behaviour personally and as a team.

---

[173] Ian Parkinson, Understanding Christian Leadership, SCM Publishing, 2020, Pg 183

Pause | Selah

"When the church really takes on the humble characteristics of Christ, that's going to lead to revival."[174]
Francis Chan

---

[174] Francis Chan, Letters to the Church, David C Cook, 2018

Questions for reflection/discussion

1. What Biblical characters can you note down that had control issues? What was behind their controlling behaviour?

2. Who released you to lead? What was it about them that enabled you to step into this well?

3. As a team, who could you be releasing to lead in your context right now?

4. As a team, how can you delegate responsibility not just tasks – What could this look like in practice? (Perhaps use a current scenario to help you with this.)

> *Accountability asks of another to stay and keep watch with us. To allow others to walk with us, to journey with us, to keep watch with us so that we might not fall into temptation.*

Chapter 7
Fiercely Accountable/Vulnerable

"Arrogance often shows up in leaders as the unwillingness to be checked or opposed or questioned in any way. It has been called, 'the wrongness of those who think they are always right.'"[175]

Tom Marshall

"But he said to me, 'My grace is sufficient for you, for my power is made perfect in weakness.' Therefore, I will boast all the more gladly about my weaknesses, so that Christ's power may rest on me."[176]

2 Corinthians 12:9

I'll never forget the experience when first sharing my personal struggle with lust and porn with a couple of close friends when I was a late teenager. I had lived in a world of guilt, heaviness and shame for a long time and on my return from a summer spiritual high, I knew I needed to get help, so I turned to two close friends. I can picture exactly where I was one Sunday afternoon when I finally plucked up the courage to share what was going on. I had no idea what to expect in terms of how they would react, but I knew that I really needed their support. Instead of judgement, I found grace. As I opened up

---

[175] Tom Marshall, Understanding Leadership, Baker Books, 2003

[176] Holy Bible, 2 Corinthians 12:9, New International Version®, NIV® Copyright ©1973, 1978, 1984, 2011 by Biblica

about my struggle, they too shared about how in different ways they were struggling with the same issue. We found empathy to be incredibly powerful and although we encountered grace, it was not a grace that said, "It's all ok" but a grace that said, "Let's pray for change." As we walked home we realised that we were not alone and that we could together walk each other with the Holy Spirit's help and transformation to a place of freedom. That conversation was the beginning of the journey, not the end. But as we continued to open up and share our struggles, we became accountable to one another, which enabled us to break free of unhelpful cycles in our lives. I learnt a valuable lesson that day, which was that vulnerability leads to freedom not to shame.

A few years ago, I watched a documentary about female bears trying to care for their cubs. It was amazing to watch these bears, who were incredibly vulnerable. Here they were trying to raise cubs, keeping watch for other bears who might attack the cubs at any moment at the same time as having to fish for the cub and herself so that she might gain enough weight to hibernate. It was fascinating. These bears were vulnerable, they had to have eyes in the back of their heads, danger was everywhere. Life was hanging in the balance; it was edge of your seat viewing. This level of vulnerability was scary. Surely to be vulnerable has to be a bad thing; we don't want to grow in being vulnerable and having life in the balance. What does vulnerability mean?

Letting others in: vulnerability

The Oxford Dictionary defines vulnerability as "exposed to the possibility of being harmed".[177] This suggests that vulnerability is to be in a state of high alert. The truth is that when we are real and honest about who we really are, there is always the threat of rejection, judgement, mockery even. To be vulnerable is risky. Vulnerability, in an emotional and spiritual sense, means to let people into your life. To be real is to be honest and transparent with others so we reveal who we really are instead of wearing a mask and pretending to be someone who we are not.

I spend a lot of time listening to people who share their challenges and problems. What I've discovered is that we are all broken. We've all got things we are ashamed of; we've all got things we struggle with, challenges in our families, times of stress and pain; hurt from past relationships and loss of loved ones. We're all broken and yet, so often in this world—and, sadly, especially within the Church—we put on a mask and pretend that everything is OK because that is what we think we should do. J. David Lundy wrote, "Transparency means being ourselves around other people. The humanity of the leader is something followers yearn to see."[178] The irony is that we so often play pretend and don't let others in as people and especially as leaders. We think we need to have it all together or others won't be able to trust us or rely on us, so we pretend. But the truth is that we all want

---

[177] https://www.oed.com/?tl=true

[178] J.David Lundy, Servant Leadership for slow learners, Authentic Lifestyle 2002

to follow those who are real, those who recognise they are broken and are vulnerable enough to admit it. Following leaders who are vulnerable and real enables and allows a community of people to be vulnerable and real. This kind of real, transparent and transformative community is what many of us deeply desire. John Owen writes, "On our own, you and I will never develop a competency for recognising our sin – We'll always need help."[179] We were never meant to do life on our own, we were made for relationship with God and others.

Jesus modelled a fierce vulnerability even within his sinless life. A great example is in the garden of Gethsemane. Here, Jesus, I believe, shows us that even though he is the Son of God, there are times when He will struggle and be overwhelmed. Here is the Messiah sent from the beginning of time to suffer and die to rescue humankind and just before the arrest, he is overwhelmed. The weight of the world is on his shoulders. On arrival in the garden, Matthew records that Jesus said to his disciples, "Sit here whilst I go over there and pray."[180] Jesus seems to want his followers close by. As he faced the most lonely and isolating moment of his life, he wanted them with him.

He takes the three (Peter, James and John) on a little further and we are told that Jesus began to be sorrowful and troubled. In this flood of emotions, Jesus chooses immediately to tell the three how he is feeling: "My soul is

---

[179] John Owen, The Mortification of Sin in believers, Ssel, 2023

[180] Holy Bible, Matthew 26:36, New International Version®, NIV® Copyright ©1973, 1978, 1984, 2011 by Biblica

overwhelmed to the point of death,"[181] and adds "Stay and keep watch." He is broken and gets his three closest disciples and shares what is going on in the inner man. Surely, the Son of God should have shown his power, his kingly strength in this moment. Instead, Jesus reveals his humanity and is vulnerable with his disciples. Of all the people, he could have worn a mask. "I'm the Son of God" he could have thought, "Pull yourself together!" In stark contrast, he fiercely and humbly shows his weakness and shares his pain. It is interesting that Jesus says, "His soul is overwhelmed to the point of death." He feels completely defeated, he is overwhelmed with what sounds like depression, deep anxiety about what is to come. We have, in Jesus, a Saviour who knows what it feels like to be completely overwhelmed, consumed with grief and suffering: "For we do not have a high priest who is unable to empathise with our weaknesses,"[182] and, "Surely he took up our pain and bore our suffering."[183]

Jesus shows here what real vulnerability looks like. A transparency and honesty that is powerful. If the Son of God needed to share his burdens with others, who are we to think we must carry them alone?

What, then, is the opposite of being vulnerable? Those of us who aren't vulnerable with others are closed, we

---

[181] Holy Bible, Matthew 26:38, New International Version®, NIV® Copyright ©1973, 1978, 1984, 2011 by Biblica

[182] Holy Bible, Hebrews 4:15, New International Version®, NIV® Copyright ©1973, 1978, 1984, 2011 by Biblica

[183] Holy Bible, Isaiah 53:4, New International Version®, NIV® Copyright ©1973, 1978, 1984, 2011 by Biblica

operate on a superficial level lacking depth and honesty. Those who aren't vulnerable have fear reigning inside, scared of other's reactions to what we share or where sin may still have power over us because we won't share it. Our pride overrules us and we'd rather be living a lie and have people think we are OK than be real and people potentially lose respect for us. The irony is that people respect those who walk with a limp more than those who have it all together. The older I become, the more I realise that those who I most respect, whose character runs deep are those who lead but have suffered and experience a dark night of the soul. Nouwen takes this personal reflection further, writing: "The great illusion of leadership is to think that man can be led out of the desert by someone who has never been there. Our lives are filled with examples which tell us that leadership asks for understanding and that understanding requires sharing. So long as we define leadership in terms of being responsible for some kind of abstract 'general good,' we have forgotten that no God can save us except a suffering God and that no man can lead his people except the man who is crushed by its sins."[184] This quote from the book 'Wounded Healer' is another reminder of the importance of vulnerability and empathy from the leader who has travelled through pain themselves and can show some empathy and understanding.

It is easy to feel, however, that we should be modelling transformed, whole lives all the time. We must learn that transformed in this life doesn't mean free from trial and pain. We must learn to humble ourselves and recognise our own need of others. Floyd McClung adds, "Others

---

[184] Henri Nouwen, Wounded Healer, Darton, Longman & Todd Ltd, 2014

fear that humility requires having their secret sins made known to one and all. Many criminals are caught and have their crimes exposed in the media, but they do not grow in humility."[185] This is a helpful thought and links back to the difference between humbling ourselves verses being humbled.

James 5:16 says, "Therefore confess your sins to each other and pray for each other so that you may be healed."[186] This is a fascinating verse: we are encouraged to confess our sins, be vulnerable and allow people to pray for us and for us to pray for others so we may be healed. Is this some clever little trick to get healed quick? No, but I believe it's saying that if we aren't prepared to share with someone that we have a problem, for example with gambling, and get some prayer, then we aren't going to stop doing it. But if people support us, pray with us and hold us to account, we might be able to stop gambling and come to a place of healing from potentially addictive behaviour.

So, what do we need to be vulnerable about? Probably, whatever comes to your mind when asked, "What do you most struggle with?" It could also include what issue you find it difficult to talk about and your relationship with Jesus, including your doubts and questions and your devotion to him.

Some people have no problems sharing with anyone and everyone their struggles. Notice that Jesus didn't run

---

[185] Floyd McClung, Whole Hearted, Harper Collins, 1988, Pg 143

[186] Holy Bible, James 5:16, New International Version®, NIV® Copyright ©1973, 1978, 1984, 2011 by Biblica

around telling everyone, he selected three who he trusted and who could walk with him. It's not appropriate to tell en masse everything you are struggling with, if you do then and it becomes attention seeking. Let me clarify, if you are worried about an exam, you can share with everyone to get them to pray, get it on a prayer chain or something similar. However, sharing with everyone deep hurt about your work colleague should be shared on a smaller scale to help you work through it. It is all about learning about appropriate sharing. The sad truth is that often the "share for prayer" mindset can kick in, which is just an excuse to sound off and gossip. This doesn't help anyone and adds further hurt and pain.

Some are the opposite and struggle to share anything with anyone; this, too, is inappropriate. If we find ourselves in that area it may be because we are more of a mental processor and don't need to talk things through with others as much. As a result, we can look on others sharing their struggles as weak or over emotional. This isn't appropriate, either. We need to humble ourselves and force ourselves out from a place of being closed and to open up with those who can help us, who we respect and who can help us to keep opening up over time. Bonhoeffer helpfully wrote, "He who denies his neighbour the service of praying for him denies him the service of a Christian."[187] Strong words for those of us who struggle to be vulnerable and ask for prayer.

Going back to Gethsemane, after Jesus was vulnerable with the disciples, he doesn't go into a big counselling session with them. Instead, he simply asks them to stay

---

[187] Dietrich Bonhoeffer, Life Together, SCM Press, 1954

with him and keep watch as he goes to the Father. He "fell with his face to the ground and prayed, 'My Father, if it is possible, may this cup be taken from me. Yet not as I will but as you will.'"[188] Jesus is vulnerable with others and also with God. We must learn how to be vulnerable and real with God. It is so easy to wear a mask, even with God, where we don't want to let Him into an area of our lives, perhaps an area of sin or pain or a dream. It's crazy when you think about it. He is the all-knowing and all-seeing God who knows us better than we know ourselves and yet we can pretend that all is well, as if he doesn't know what is really going on. Jesus pours his heart out to God, asking Him if there is another way whilst still submitting to His will.

This is a helpful example that perhaps we miss when we invite others to open up. Perhaps after a talk, we invite people to come forward for prayer or simply in a one-to-one interaction in a coffee shop with a friend. It is so easy to talk about the issue, to share advice about the issue but not to take the issue to God together. I regularly, when people come forward to pray, simply invite people to tell God what they want to tell Him when they have shared, simply invite them to be real with God, then I will pray for them and simply invite God to meet with them rather than trying to resolve the issue myself. Of course, there is often a need for counselling which can be so important and necessary to bring change in someone's life, but as we pray for people, we should encourage vulnerability with God first rather than trying to fix it ourselves.

---

[188] Holy Bible, Matthew 26:39, New International Version®, NIV® Copyright ©1973, 1978, 1984, 2011 by Biblica

Jesus showed us a fierce vulnerability that calls us to do the same. The disciples weren't very good at standing with him when he needed them, they fell asleep! Hopefully, none of us will experience that when we ask others to watch and pray with us! Jesus shows that we need each other. We were created for relationship with God that is deep and rich and real and, also, we were made for relationship with other humans, which should also be deep and rich and real. Imagine if we, as the Church, can limp together towards God, being real with each other about our struggles, our temptations, our hurts and pain whilst not being content with these things but seeking God for wholeness and breakthrough together. What a safe place that would be and it would be so attractive to people outside because they are craving reality, fed up with gimmicks and hypocrisy and fake lives.

Accountability – Submitting to others

To be simply vulnerable is important, but that vulnerability should lead to accountability. To be accountable can be defined as "subject to the obligation to report, explain, or justify something; responsible; answerable".[189] To be accountable is to submit ourselves to others, it is to allow them to question us and to challenge us. Simon Walker in his book 'Undefended Leader' says, "Accountability and submission are crucial factors in leadership: no leader should be without them."[190]

---

[189] https://www.dictionary.com/browse/accountable#

[190] Simon Walker, Leading out of who you are, Piquant Editions, 2007

We, again, see in the life of Jesus a fierce humility that is accountable and submitted to others. In Luke 2:51 it says, "Then he went down to Nazareth with them and was obedient to them."[191] Jesus submitted to his parents. This is a part of just two verses that cover from Jesus being a boy until he is baptised and starts his ministry. He submits to them. Jesus, as mentioned in the chapter on fiercely relying on the Father, submitted completely to God. He showed us what it means to be submitted and accountable to God. Returning to Gethsemane, Jesus showed the path of vulnerability and also the path of accountability as he says, "Stay and keep watch."[192] In this moment of deep suffering, Jesus asks them to stay with him. He needed them at this moment and asked them to stay in his darkest hour so that he might not be physically alone. Accountability asks of another to stay and keep watch with us. To allow others to walk with us, to journey with us, to keep watch with us so that we might not fall into temptation.

What is the opposite to being accountable? To not be accountable is to have to work everything out on your own; it is independence and self-reliance. This can happen because of a fear of letting others in or pride reigning through a belief that we don't need others.

If we want to seek fierce humility, we must humble ourselves before others and invite them to speak into our lives. Proverbs 27:17 says, "As iron sharpens iron, so one

---

[191] Holy Bible, Luke 2 v 51, New International Version®, NIV® Copyright ©1973, 1978, 1984, 2011 by Biblica

[192] Holy Bible, Matthew 26 v 38, New International Version®, NIV® Copyright ©1973, 1978, 1984, 2011 by Biblica

person sharpens another."[193] This verse encourages relationships where we are sharpened and help sharpen one another. These are relationships of accountability. Paul also encourages us in Ephesians 5:21: "Submit to one another out of reverence to Christ."[194] CJ Maloney writes, "The practice of guarding each other is clearly a biblical practice. It's a gift from God, a vital means of experiencing His grace for protection from the deceitfulness of sin."[195] If accountability is biblical and modelled by Jesus, then how do we do it and do it well?

Accountability in life

We need to seek out accountability intentionally. Accountability doesn't present itself before you. We need to find those we can ask and can meet up with to talk honestly about life. Seek out one to three people to walk with you in the highs and lows of life. Maybe a prayer triplet or a mentor or, even better, both! You are looking for those who can be objective, who are wise, who can give us godly advice and practical help. Don't gather people who will just excuse what you are doing, find someone who you are slightly scared of and you know will push you to change and move on and grow. Tom

---

[193] Holy Bible, Proverbs 27 v 17, New International Version®, NIV® Copyright ©1973, 1978, 1984, 2011 by Biblica

[194] Holy Bible, Ephesians 5 v 21, New International Version®, NIV® Copyright ©1973, 1978, 1984, 2011 by Biblica

[195] C.J.Mahaney, Humility - True Greatness, Soverign Grace Ministries, 2005, Pg 117

Marshall writes, "Seeking to learn from others and aspiring to emulate good role models are signs of healthy humility."[196]

These questions from CJ Maloney are both challenging and helpful, exploring how we can sometimes think we are being accountable, but we are not: "If you're in a small group for fellowship and accountability, are you humbly and aggressively participating or merely observing? Are you hoping to avoid correction? Do you experience a certain perverse relief when your sin has gone undetected? Are you regularly informing others of your temptations and sins, or do you present to them a carefully edited and flattering version of yourself?"[197]

These questions make sure you are not just pretending to be accountable whilst really continuing to be closed off to others. Ultimately, if you want to grow, you must walk in accountable relationships. John Wesley, in 1729, started a club with his brother, Charles, called 'The Holy Club' where they had 22 questions to ask each other.[198] The questions gave no room for wriggling out of answering honestly. They were direct and clear. I often ask those who want me to hold them accountable over something, what question I should ask them. I ask this so that they come up with a similar feature of something direct and

---

[196] Tom Marshall, Understanding Leadership, Baker Books, 2003

[197] C.J.Mahaney, Humility - True Greatness, Soverign Grace Ministries, 2005, Pg 129

[198] https://www.umcdiscipleship.org/resources/everyday-disciples-john-wesleys-22-questions

confrontational which will get a truthful answer. Some of the 'Holy Clubs' questions included:

- Am I consciously or unconsciously creating the impression that I am better than I really am? In other words, Am I a hypocrite?

- Do I confidentially pass on to others what has been said to me in confidence?

- Do I give the Bible time to speak to me every day?

- When did I last speak to someone else of my faith?

- Am I jealous, impure, critical, irritable, touchy or distrustful?

They are challenging and, still, very relevant questions nearly two hundred years on. You can see how answering these questions every day would propel you forwards. The key to using questions like this would be to be surrounded by grace and encouragement so it does not fall into a legalistic, shame-based activity.

My experience in accountability groups is that the key is to meet as regularly as possible and try to avoid, at all costs, getting complacent, but to continue to ask difficult questions. Take turns encouraging and praying for each other. It is only God who can bring the change in us we desire, so accountability should be surrounded in prayer. We all need accountability, which is made more impactful through real vulnerability together.

Accountability in our role

As Christians, we should be seeking accountability in our lives; we must also seek to be accountable and submit to others within whatever leadership role we are carrying out. Whether church leader, worship team leader, charity leader or small group leader, you should always have someone to submit to and to whom you can be accountable.

Terms such as "maverick" or "lone ranger" are sometimes used around leaders who refuse to make themselves accountable to people around them. Those who find themselves in positions of leadership have a choice to be placed under others or to avoid this as much as possible. Whether that accountability is a PCC, a trustee board or a group of elders, we need those who can call us to account on our leadership. Tom Marshall writes, "Without the acid of objective questioning to keep us in touch with reality, we can be led astray by distorted perceptions, grandiose delusions, poor judgement or faulty discernment. But it is such critical examination that arrogance resents most bitterly and rejects most indignantly."[199]

Pride chooses to reject what is perceived as interference or negative criticism from others. Pride gets defensive and takes criticism personally, so instead of humbly submitting to others, it chooses to control and close down open relationships with the people above. Often, pride in leaders causes them to only place "yes" people around them. This can even happen subconsciously as leaders place those who will agree with them or would

---

[199] Tom Marshall, Understanding Leadership, Baker Books, 2003

never challenge them in positions of accountability. We need to make a conscious choice to make sure we have those who have strong opinions who will challenge us. This does not mean just appointing difficult, opinionated people but choosing strong, wise, prayerful and discerning people who will speak up for what they believe to be right before God. Tom Marshall continues, "The more successful we are as leaders, the more we need our critics, even when they are wrong, because at the very least they help to save us from the dangers of arrogance."[200]

I've been involved in the same charity now for so long that I've had several line managers and have seen our board of trustees change during my time. Our trustees are amazing: they are a brilliant group of encouraging, supportive and wise people from a variety of backgrounds. Over the years, several chairpeople have fostered a culture of releasing and not controlling the staff whilst caring deeply and providing solid questioning and accountability to the team on the ground. As I have been involved for a long time, when we are looking for new trustees, people now ask me who I think would be good to get involved. We try and have a diversity of people and I now class all the board members my friends; however, not all are "yes" people. Many have vastly different opinions to me on everything from theology to how things should be worked out in practice. I value and enjoy that we can have strong and robust conversations within a culture of trust where we never fall out but are able to wrestle with difficult issues and decisions. I have seen trustee boards or accountability structures that are far

---

[200] Tom Marshall, Understanding Leadership, Baker Books, 2003

from this, either suffocating the leader, saying 'yes' to everything with no challenge, or so disengaged they are almost non-existent. Whatever our accountability structure or the person who we report to, our role as a leader is to seek to submit to them which includes doing what they ask even when we disagree.

Jesus modelled fierce vulnerability and accountability in his life and ministry so how do we lead our teams in the same way? How do we encourage vulnerability and accountability in our teams?

1. Make space for real conversation in your team

It is very easy to be very task-centred and focused on delivering what we are setting out as a team to deliver. It doesn't take much to form a habit of asking people to share in a group how they are doing. Throwing a couple of thought-provoking questions in to encourage honest conversation and having time to pray before entering into the activity you are involved in. This could be for ten minutes before running the children's group or for twenty minutes at the start of a leadership meeting. Of course, a group environment might be a bit too intimating for some to be able to be vulnerable so occasionally splitting off into pairs or male and female small groups can be helpful too.

We are looking for opportunities for honest and open conversation as being normal and encouraged. A key way to practice fierce humility in this area is to model vulnerability and accountability to your team and encourage them to do the same. This requires appropriate sharing of areas you are struggling with or asking the team to pray for you. Occasionally you can show that this is not only OK for them to do so, but something that is normal and encouraged. As a part of this, you could share about those you are accountable too and encourage your team to have a mentor or accountability group as a part of your team values. Speaking well of those to whom you are accountable is important, so developing healthy relationships with your team and those over you can be important, too. Another way to model fierce humility is to welcome critique from those inside and outside your circle of influence.

2. Line manage those you are responsible for well

Over the years at SWYM, we have learnt the hard way that expecting people to line manage well is a bad idea. I've had several church leaders tell me that our training on line-management was the first they'd ever had in years of church leadership, when line-managing staff and volunteers. The danger is that we think that we can hold people accountable by grabbing the odd conversation here and there at events, church etc. Nothing helps good communication, clear expectations and feedback than sitting down for a focused conversation. I prefer keeping notes to refer back to. You might be thinking this is too formal, especially with volunteers, but a regular check-in to see how people are getting on and to encourage and thank them helps you to value your team. It's often busyness that inhibits us from line managing well, but in my experience giving the time to regular line management saves time in the long run. Hanson and Hanson helpfully reflect "creating a culture of integrity and accountability not only improves effectiveness, but it also generates a respectful, enjoyable and life-giving setting in which to work".[201] I don't know about you, but that's the kind of setting I want to create for my team.

---

[201] Hanson and Hanson, Who will do what by when?, Power Publications/ Hanson House, 2010

Pause | Selah

The wind is howling like this swirling storm inside. Couldn't keep it in, heaven knows I've tried. Don't let them in, don't let them see. Be the good girl you always have to be. Conceal, don't feel, don't let them know. Well, now they know

Let it go, let it go. Can't hold it back anymore. Let it go, let it go. Turn away and slam the door. I don't care what they're going to say. Let the storm rage on. The cold never bothered me anyway

Let it Go – Frozen[202]

---

[202] Kristen Jane Anderson-Lopez / Robert Joseph Lopez, Let it Go, Universal Music Publishing Group, 2013

Questions for reflection/discussion

1. When did you last ask someone to pray for you or ask someone to help you? What does this tell you about yourself?

2. Who are you accountable to? How vulnerable are you with them? What needs to change to make these relationships more real?

3. Who are you accountable to functionally? What does submitting to them look like for you? Do you ever manipulate them to get your way?

4. What practical first steps are you going to take to foster vulnerability in your team

Practising forgiveness takes emotional energy; it requires working through the pain, the awkwardness, confronting another and ultimately humbling ourselves.

Chapter 8
Fiercely Forgiving

"May God teach us that our thoughts, words and feelings concerning our fellow man are His test of our humility towards Him."[203]

Andrew Murray

"Do not judge and you will not be judged. Do not condemn and you will not be condemned. Forgive and you will be forgiven."[204]

Luke 6:37

When I was about fourteen or fifteen years old, I used to take a long daily bus ride to and from school. The bus home would start pretty full when leaving school and gradually empty until there were only two stops left. There was another teenager, who we will call Bob for the purpose of this story. Bob was a part of the cool gang in the year group. You know the type? We had an unwritten agreement that meant that we never spoke at school or on the bus until it was just the two of us left on board. When we got to this point, I would head to the back of the bus, or he would move towards the front and we would chat. We would talk about school, football... anything

---

[203] Andrew Murray, Humility – The Beauty of Holiness, Aneko Press, Revised Edition, 2016, Pg 43

[204] Holy Bible, Luke 6:37, New International Version®, NIV® Copyright ©1973, 1978, 1984, 2011 by Biblica

really. It was a strange sort of friendship, but it worked and we were both happy with it.

One day he asked me if I fancied the girl that everyone in the year group thought was the most attractive girl in the year. I knew she was out of my league and never would have thought about it, but I agreed with him that I thought she was attractive. A few days later, I sat down on the bus at the end of a long day at school and waited for the journey to begin when, suddenly, Bob got on the bus and called my name. This was very strange. What did he want? Why was he communicating with me now? This was outside of our normal parameters. He asked me to get off the bus for a moment. I was intrigued and slightly scared but agreed. I stepped off the bus and there were a group of around eight to ten of the cool group, including this girl. He called me over with several of the lads laughing. Then Bob said to me, "Go on then. Ask her out. Go on ask her." I was mortified and didn't know what to do. He continued, "Do you really think she would go out with you?" I could tell the girl was finding this awkward, although not as awkward as I was. I turned around and headed back to the bus, my face growing more and more red with each step. My friendship with Bob had been undermined for a quick laugh and I was humiliated.

This was one of my first real forgiveness challenges. I couldn't pretend everything was OK, but I had to see this guy every day. Our strange friendship was never the same, but I had to learn that even though he wasn't repentant, I needed to forgive if I was going to be able to function on this bus journey for the following years.

Forgiveness is hard. Both asking for forgiveness when we hurt others and, in my experience, even harder when having to forgive others. I have always found that knowing we are forgiven aids the process in both circumstances.

The astounding forgiveness and mercy of God revealed in Jesus

The most quoted phrase in the Old Testament—used nine times and therefore probably used as a part of worship during Hebraic worship—is this beautiful description of the character of God. He is described as "gracious and compassionate, slow to anger, abounding in loving kindness".[205] The beloved disciple John later describes God as "love" but here we get a more detailed description, showing that God is gracious and compassionate towards His people. He is not quick to judge or to be angry but is abounding in loving kindness. The Old Testament tells us about the character of God and the New Testament shows evidence of it through the actions of Jesus.

If we ever lose a sense of wonder at the grace and mercy of God towards us, we need to head back to the foot of the Cross. It is God's nature to forgive, to reconcile and we, as the recipients of that forgiveness, are so undeserving of all that he showers on us.

In Isaiah 1:18 we read, "Come now, let us reason together, says the Lord: though your sins are like scarlet, they shall be as white as snow; though they are red like crimson,

---

[205] Holy Bible, Psalm 103:8, New International Version®, NIV® Copyright ©1973, 1978, 1984, 2011 by Biblica

they shall become like wool."[206] God desired a coming together, to cleanse and renew us. Daniel 9:9 says, "To the Lord our God belong mercy and forgiveness, for we have rebelled against him."[207] Mercy and forgiveness are His. He created them, He possesses them and because of our rebellion against Him and our wilful turning away from Him, He has turned towards us in mercy and forgiveness. Finally, Psalm 103:2 says, "As far as the East is from the West, so far does he remove our transgressions from us."[208] What an incredible verse. We are told that when God forgives, He completely removes, He doesn't hold our sin against us, He is not guarded or untrusting towards us, He completely removes our transgressions from us. God is gracious and compassionate which leads him to forgive the unforgivable, to remove our guilt and shame. What a gift to be free from sin, to be cleansed, renewed, restored, forgiven. Of course, this was all achieved for us at the Cross and the empty tomb and we see this astounding forgiveness displayed for all to see as he hangs and fiercely forgives.

In Luke 23:34, it records that Jesus said, "Father, forgive them, for they do not know what they are

---

[206] Holy Bible, Isaiah 1:18, New International Version®, NIV® Copyright ©1973, 1978, 1984, 2011 by Biblica

[207] Holy Bible, Daniel 9:9, New International Version®, NIV® Copyright ©1973, 1978, 1984, 2011 by Biblica

[208] Holy Bible, Psalm 103:12, New International Version®, NIV® Copyright ©1973, 1978, 1984, 2011 by Biblica

doing."[209] During the ultimate rejection, pain, loneliness and isolation, Jesus prays for others. He could have prayed, "Father, help me" or "Father, give me strength" but, instead, he prayed "forgive them". Jesus was modelling what he had previously taught: "Love your enemies and pray for those that persecute you."[210] John Wesley said, "While they are nailing him to the cross, he seems to feel the injury they did to their own souls more than the wounds they gave him."[211]

In this prayer at his last hour, Jesus addresses the God of the Universe with the simple term "Father". When we have been hurt and don't know how to forgive, we can go to God as our Daddy; we are seeking help, justice and grace. We can come as Jesus did to our Father.

"Forgive them."[212] Who is them? As Jesus hung on the Cross looking out at the crowd, perhaps he was referring to the guards standing there; perhaps it was the chief priests and scribes mocking him; perhaps it was Pilate who sentenced him; or perhaps he was thinking of all humanity, including you and I, all for whom he was dying to save. Whether it was one or all of these, what we do

---

[209] Holy Bible, Luke 23:34, New International Version®, NIV® Copyright ©1973, 1978, 1984, 2011 by Biblica

[210] Holy Bible, Matthew 5:44, New International Version®, NIV® Copyright ©1973, 1978, 1984, 2011 by Biblica

[211] John Wesley's Explanatory Notes, 1755

[212] Holy Bible, Luke 23:34, New International Version®, NIV® Copyright ©1973, 1978, 1984, 2011 by Biblica

know is that in this moment of deep pain he chooses to forgive.

Jesus fiercely forgave in a moment that many would have given him permission to be self-focused. He humbled himself to think of others. The graciousness of God, the compassion and loving kindness of God, fleshed out in a prayer as the Son of God died for us all. If and when we are struggling to forgive, it is helpful to go back to the Cross, to remember how much we have been forgiven. Perhaps even reflecting on all he has wiped away in our own lives, what he has washed away from our hearts. Reflecting on his loving-kindness towards us can and should motivate us to want to continue the flow of forgiveness towards those who have wronged us.

Our call to make the first move towards right relationship

When we feel under threat, we naturally move into fight or flight mode. In conflict, we often make the situation worse if we go into fight mode as we go on the defensive or attack the other person. If we veer towards flight, then we alternatively just run away from the conflict and the threat of further pain. People move on from one church to another for lots of different reasons, but the main reason is because of relational fall out. It is easier to cut and run rather than work through relational tension. People are problematic and we find it easier to move on than to work through forgiveness. We are all, I'd like to argue, called to make the first move towards the right relationship. Too often, I've heard people upset or unable to forgive because they are waiting for the other person to make the first move. They are unwilling to start the journey because "they haven't said sorry to me" or "they haven't spoken to me about it at all". Whatever the situation, it is ours, mine and your responsibility to make the first move.

Asking for forgiveness: In Matthew 5, Jesus explains that when we are in the wrong, we must go and ask for forgiveness. "Therefore, if you are offering your gift at the altar and there, remember that your brother or sister has something against you, leave your gift there in front of the altar. First, go and be reconciled to them; then come and offer your gift."[213] Jesus is explaining here that if we have wronged others we should not go to God as if everything is fine; we should go and resolve it and ask for forgiveness first. This is clearly important to God that we resolve hurt we have caused to others. Jesus is teaching us that it is our job to initiate forgiveness.

I've never found it particularly hard to say sorry, perhaps this is because I'm a master of manipulation or just that I'm in the wrong a lot! Whatever the reason, it is definitely a word leaders must learn to say and say often—and be first to say it. The word "sorry" is an admission of guilt, admitting fault. Some of us don't like admitting fault. Most conflict is a strange mix of fault being with both parties, to a greater or lesser degree, but this doesn't mean we aren't the first to take responsibility for our part in this.

Forgiveness is tough. I am the father of two boys and when they were smaller, I sometimes had to take on the role of referee. Imagine, for a moment, two young children happily playing a game with lots of laughter, then

---

[213] Holy Bible, Matthew 5:23-24, New International Version®, NIV® Copyright ©1973, 1978, 1984, 2011 by Biblica

suddenly the laughter changes: one gets too rough, the other moves from a friendly tap on the arm to a full-on wallop. The other's immediate reaction is to return the favour. In thirty-seconds, the scene has turned from a lovely moment to tears, upset and fall out. Into this situation steps the dad or referee.

Firstly, I need to listen to what has happened, hearing from both on their view of what happened, managing my way through the "he started it" accusations and to help them to get to a position of being willing to apologise for their part in it. I have learnt the hard way: that forcing someone to say sorry can be dangerous, as it can breed non-genuine behaviour where we learn to say the words without our heart being in agreement. Asking someone to forgive us is humbling, saying sorry and meaning it isn't easy. It takes practice and is something that if we want to be leaders, we must be quick to say and mean it. If we want to create Christ-like communities, we must be those who model forgiveness, who are quick to say sorry and quick to forgive those who wrong us. Billy Graham commented that after we have asked someone for forgiveness: "You will have done everything you could to let them know you regret what happened and that you want their forgiveness. That's what's important to God."[214] Of course, people might refuse to forgive, but that isn't our responsibility, it is for us to seek their forgiveness leaving them with the decision to receive it or not.

Practising forgiveness takes emotional energy; it requires working through the pain, the awkwardness, confronting

---

[214] https://billygraham.org.uk/answer/seek-the-forgiveness-of-those-youve-hurt/

another and ultimately humbling ourselves. As a leader, I have to not only say sorry to people for the things I've done wrong, but for the things that my team or organisation/church has done wrong. I've learnt to take responsibility for hurt caused and mistakes made, even if it was nothing to do with me. This is humbling but absolutely necessary—even if we did nothing wrong. As a result of what was done, someone has been hurt and we need to apologise for that and talk it through with that person. Asking for forgiveness is something that, if we are not able to manage, will leave a trail of broken relationships or hurt behind us. Saying sorry builds a bridge and creates a path to forgiveness.

Forgiving others: Matthew 18:15 starts, "If your brother or sister sins, go and point out their fault, just between the two of you."[215] We have seen that if we sin against someone, we need to seek forgiveness from them; but here we see that if someone else sins against us we once again are instructed to go to them. Jesus seems to be saying that there is no circumstance where we get to sit back and wait for someone else to resolve the issue. If you were in the wrong, go and put it right; if someone else was in the wrong go and put it right.

Clearly, disunity and relational fall-out had such a potential to rip apart communities that Jesus lays a foundation for conflict: not dealing with it should not be tolerated. Tom Marshall, when speaking about this comments on Matthew 18, when he wrote, "Jesus says that if my brother sins against me, I am still the one who

---

[215] Holy Bible, Matthew 18:15, New International Version®, NIV® Copyright ©1973, 1978, 1984, 2011 by Biblica

has to take the initiative to show him his fault and try to win him. He may be bound and burdened with guilt and because I do not have guilt to struggle against, I can act more freely and more graciously than he can to achieve reconciliation."[216] This is a helpful point to recognise, that sometimes it is easier to approach another to find forgiveness and build a bridge. We see Jesus demonstrate this with Peter, as Jesus, who was the one who has been hurt and betrayed, cooks Peter breakfast and invites him to come and be reconciled. What a brilliant picture of what we should do when we are hurt. We have a choice to run and gossip or to make a metaphorical breakfast and make a space to reconcile with that person.

Paul, in Romans, uses a phrase that I find so helpful when he wrote, "If it is possible, as far as it depends on you, live at peace with everyone."[217] This is excellent relational advice. Paul is encouraging us to work hard at living in the right relationship with those around us. The fact that Paul advises "if it is possible" suggests that sometimes it is not. Sometimes, others will never forgive or step towards a right relationship, it may be impossible because you cannot control the heart of the other. Paul adds "as far as it depends on you"; in other words, do everything you can to bring healing, forgive and forgive and forgive. Work at it, work through the awkwardness, humble yourself before them, do all you can possibly do

---

[216] Tom Marshall, Understanding Leadership, Baker Books, 2003

[217] Holy Bible, Romans 12:18, New International Version®, NIV® Copyright ©1973, 1978, 1984, 2011 by Biblica

to 'live at peace with one another.' I find this verse so freeing.

I don't have a huge trail of broken relationships behind me, I'm very glad to say, but I can think of two or three times when things have got incredibly emotionally difficult with a lot of hurt going both ways. I have in all these cases tried as best I can with the Holy Spirit's help to "as far as it depends on me to live at peace" with them. In some cases, it has been impossible; I've not seen them again, they moved away or there were other issues. Over time, I've seen change and healing in my own heart and with them, but this has taken time. In a couple of cases, it is totally out of my control if I ever hear from them again, but I can, hand on heart, say I couldn't have done any more to try and resolve and work this through.

The truth is that it takes guts to make the first move towards the right relationship. I'm a conflict avoider if I'm being honest. Growing up, my family's way of dealing with conflict was that if someone was upset you would disappear off in a sulk, sort yourself out and come back when you were OK and carry on as if nothing had ever happened. I can remember being very shocked when I first stayed with my wife Jo's family. Within two minutes, she and her sister were having a shouting match and then made up over a tiny issue. I realised we all have our conflict resolution history and background, for better or worse, but if like me you recognise you are a conflict avoider, then you need to "put on your big boy or big girl pants" and learn to humble yourself when faced with broken relationships.

It would seem that from Scripture all of us are instructed to deal with conflict whoever "started it" and to go after the right relationship. I believe, however, that as leaders, this call to address issues, deal with tension before it bursts into full-on conflict is our responsibility. Sometimes, we have to act like a mum or dad and get people together to help them sort things out; we do whatever we can to make sure that we work through conflict, not avoiding it. Often, the challenge for us is that forgiving someone once is possible for most of us, but when people continue to hurt us, it gets more challenging.

Jesus, though, speaks about this as well in Luke 17:3–4 when he says, "If your brother sins, rebuke him and if he repents, forgive him and if he sins against you seven times in the day and turns to you seven times, saying, 'I repent,' you must forgive him."[218] This is a tough call that may require help from others and, of course, sometimes we can forgive. But we need to, for our own safety, remove the level of relationship to protect ourselves. Jesus is laying down an encouragement to forgive just as we have been forgiven.

Murray makes a really challenging point here about humility and dealing with those we find difficult: "Let us look at every person who annoys or agitates us, as God's means of grace, God's instrument for our purification, for the working out of the humility Jesus our Life breathes within us."[219] What a great way to view those we find difficult: to recognise them as an opportunity for us to humble ourselves and to know something more of the

---

[218] Holy Bible, Luke 17:3–4, New International Version®, NIV® Copyright ©1973, 1978, 1984, 2011 by Biblica

[219] Andrew Murray, Humility – The Beauty of Holiness, Aneko Press, Revised Edition, 2016, Pg 37

grace of God and the transformation He wants to bring in our hearts. Perhaps one of the most challenging verses on forgiveness is, again, from the mouth of Jesus when he says, "For if you forgive others their trespasses, your heavenly Father will also forgive you, but if you do not forgive others their trespasses, neither will your Father forgive your trespasses."[220] There are lots of different views on what this verse means theologically but taking it simply at face value, we see here just how serious unforgiveness is to our God. We are not given any wriggle room; we are simply commanded to forgive. This is not meant to make us guilty and to beat ourselves up over those we are struggling to forgive, but asking ourselves if we are walking towards forgiveness even if we are not quite there yet. Forgiveness takes time but I'd suggest we all know if we are hard-hearted and unwilling to forgive, or if we are open and tentatively walking the fragile path of forgiveness.

If leaders harbour unforgiveness to another, become bitter, doing down others out of hurt, what will those who are following do? Exactly the same, of course. Seeing forgiveness worked through and worked out is a beautiful thing. People humbling themselves and coming together in compassion and care for one another to work through and move past the pain is powerful. Henri Nouwen wrote, "Thus the authority of compassion is the possibility of man to forgive his brother because forgiveness is only real for him who has discovered the weakness of his friends and the sins of his enemy in his own heart and is

---

[220] Holy Bible, Matthew 6:14–15, New International Version®, NIV® Copyright ©1973, 1978, 1984, 2011 by Biblica

willing to call every human being his brother."[221] It is very easy during pain to make the one who has caused us pain completely evil. They are "all wrong" when, of course, the truth is they are human, they make mistakes and they also are made in the image of God. That doesn't mean they will walk towards forgiveness and reconciliation. It is good to remember to ask God to show us the good in those we are struggling with to humanise them again rather than objectify them because of the pain they have caused us.

Jesus taught about forgiveness a lot because, I'd suggest, he knew it was so critical to the future of his Church. We will explore this further in the next chapter but, ultimately, all of this teaching from Jesus pointed to his statement in John 13:35: "By this everyone will know that you are my disciples, if you love one another."[222] The world would know who followed Jesus not based on their excellent preaching, their events or festivals, but by the way they love one another. And to love also means how we continue to love and, therefore, forgive one another. Proverbs puts it well when it says: "Love prospers when a fault is forgiven, but dwelling on it separates close friends."[223] How practically do we walk the path of forgiveness? What do we do if we are struggling with this in an area of our lives?

---

[221] Henri Nouwen, Wounded Healer, Darton, Longman & Todd Ltd, 2014

[222] Holy Bible, John 13:35, New International Version®, NIV® Copyright ©1973, 1978, 1984, 2011 by Biblica

[223] Holy Bible, Proverbs 17:9, New Living Translation, Copyright © 1996, 2004, 2015 by Tyndale House Foundation

Practical steps

When you know you have wronged someone however big or small, you must be quick to put it right. Often, it can be tempting to think or even say, "Oh it was nothing"; "They know I was only joking"; 'I didn't mean it like that'. We must learn to take responsibility, to say the words, "I'm sorry" and not "I'm sorry but..." Benjamin Franklin famously said, "Never ruin an apology with an excuse."[224] We need to own our error and/or hurt caused. We have to start by lowering ourselves, get off your high horse and put yourself in their shoes, in their seat. We have to learn to let go of our defensiveness and our need to be right. When wronged, you have to do exactly the same: humble yourself, put yourself in their shoes, asking questions such as, "Did they mean it in the way we received it?" "What was going on for them in that moment?" Humbling yourself is an active first choice. Part of humbling ourselves is going to God our Father and seeking his perspective, humbling ourselves before Him and before the person who you have hurt or who has hurt you.

Speak Up: Once we have humbled ourselves you need to speak up. Speaking up means saying sorry to them or speaking up and saying, "When you said this, did this, it hurt me because... It made me feel like this..." Some people would rather live with the hurt than confront the person. If we never confront, all our relationships will be shallow, lacking any depth and we won't really be known. Unresolved conflict, pain and unforgiveness eats away at your heart. Get it sorted or it will become a stumbling

---

[224] https://www.wecreateloyalty.com/the-art-of-a-sincere-apology/

block for you. It will stop you growing, unforgiveness grows eventually into anger and bitterness. Do you know anyone in your life who is bitter? Bitterness is ugly, isn't it? I don't want to be with people who are bitter, it brings you down. Marianne Williamson said, "Unforgiveness is like drinking poison yourself and waiting for the other person to die."[225] We must speak up and get the conversation started.

One small caveat is if speaking up puts you in danger. Full reconciliation for you might not be safe. This is not an excuse to not deal with it but might require forgiving from a distance, perhaps writing a letter rather than face to face. This is rare in the forgiveness stakes I'd like to suggest and is usually found where severe abuse has been caused.

Pray for them: Once you have spoken up, you pray and keep praying for them. Forgiveness is birthed out of praying for your enemies, giving it to God, praying blessing over those we are struggling with. Unforgiveness can't cope with praying blessing, it's how you begin to break the power of it.

I have a little prayer book that I use each day to help me to pray. At various points, I've had someone in that book that I am choosing to forgive. I write a short prayer next to their name that I pray each day. It is usually something to do with blessing this person, encouraging them, strengthening them in every way, their family and work. As a part of this prayer, I will choose to lay down any bad feeling in my heart, any anger or distrust and ask God to

---

[225] Marianne Williamson, https://www.christiantoday.com/article/forgiveness.why.holding.onto.that.grudge.will.only.hurt.you/83008.htm

free me from this. I find this helpful and then, one day, I will know that I hold nothing against this person anymore; I can then move on. A good test I've discovered if you have forgiven someone is that when you bump into them or meet them you are pleased to see them and hold nothing against them. A few times I've experienced this and it has been such a joy to me to know that I've moved from unforgiveness to the freedom of forgiveness.

Prayer changes your heart and changing your heart can change your mind about people.

Shut up and speak well: Once you have put a conflict right, you have to stop talking about it. Don't go over it again and again in your mind. Forgiveness isn't an act, it's a process, the process takes longer if you keep reliving it and reliving your pain and your sense of injustice. You have to practice speaking well of the people, not allowing gossip or negativity to spread, not leading others to take sides but going after reconciliation, pushing through the awkwardness and seeking restoration and good relationship again. Proverbs 17:9 puts it so well: "Whoever covers an offence seeks love, but he who repeats a matter separates close friends."[226] I love a good story and have been known to exaggerate when telling them to make it sound even better. It's amazing when you retell a circumstance where you were hurt how quickly the story of what you felt happened, or what the other person said gets changed with further words added, or you add an interpretation. You have to be so careful. This doesn't mean you can't share with one or two who can help you

---

[226] Holy Bible, Proverbs 17 v 9, English Standard Version Copyright © 2001 by Crossway Bibles

walk towards forgiveness, but we need to be careful not to cause others to stumble.

I've seen too many leaders not deal with stuff and hurt others, themselves and their families because they could not stop trying to control their pain and let others and God in to bring the healing. Blanchard, Hodges and Hendry wrote, "When leaders are filled with pride or fear, they react to things that happen to them... They shoot from the hip and sometimes end up shooting themselves in the foot."[227] It is easy when reading this to think of others we know who we have seen do this, but it is important to look inward first. You can, I'm sure, identify times when you've sounded off to the wrong people, over-shared and dug a deeper hole as a result. A lack of self-control can lead to an outburst of anger that creates further pain.

It is so easy after the event to win people to your side by defending yourself to all around you. This can quickly cause increased conflict and fall out. It is, of course, in some senses natural to want to protect yourself, but whenever you do this, Kendell suggests, "But there are two things that are absolutely forbidden: (1) to promote yourself or (2) to clear your name."[228] It is tempting to want to clear your name but Kendell makes it very clear that this is not yours to do.

---

[227] Blanchard, Hodges and Hendry, Lead like Jesus Revisited, W Publishing, 2016

[228] R.T Kendall, The Power of Humility, Charisma House, 2011, Pg 124

Jesus fiercely forgave. He chose to humble himself and forgive and he calls us to do the same. But how do we help our teams to be settings of fierce forgiveness?

Fiercely forgiving in our teams

1. **Modelling forgiveness—asking and receiving:** Not allowing broken relationships to take root in your team. This means personally making sure you are quick to say sorry when in the wrong. Others will follow your lead, so being quick to recognise where you got it wrong and put it right, as well as quick to address any hurt or disagreement with honest conversation is important. It is also important to keep your ears to the ground for any angst or upset between members of your team, encouraging them to talk to each other and address things as they come up. If you can get your teams to address the little issues, then it is less likely that a big issue will blow up.

2. **No room for gossip:** Ultimately, you will create a culture that either breeds honest conversation or a culture that breeds fake relationships, where talking behind each other's backs becomes the norm. If you see or hear gossip, you must call it out and nip it in the bud. Nothing kills effective teams more than gossip and distrust. Make it clear early on that gossip is not allowed and then help people walk in the way of honest, helpful conversations together.

3. **Build new bridges:** Sometimes you find that people won't work with some people because of past issues or fall out. Wouldn't it be great if, as a leader, you could not just create healthy cultures of fierce

forgiveness but could take back lost ground from previous generations when unforgiveness had won? Practically this might mean reaching out to another church who you don't work with to try and forge a new relationship of trust or invite that volunteer who fell out with the last leader as a redemptive act. Going back to help others walk the path of forgiveness who thought it was all lost is a privilege and feels like you are rewriting history. Where, I wonder, in your context could you build some new bridges?

FIERCE HUMILITY

Pause | Selah

These are the few ways we can practice humility: To speak as little as possible of one's self. To mind one's own business. Not to want to manage other people's affairs. To avoid curiosity. To accept contradictions and correction cheerfully. To pass over the mistakes of others. To accept insults and injuries. To accept being slighted, forgotten and disliked. To be kind and gentle even under provocation. Never to stand on one's dignity. To choose always the hardest.

Mother Teresa[229]

---

[229] https://www.goodreads.com/quotes/663304-these-are-the-few-ways-we-can-practice-humility-to

Questions for reflection/discussion

1. Is there anyone I need to ask for forgiveness from?
2. Is there unforgiveness in me that I'm not intentionally working through? Are there broken relationships/people I'm avoiding from either my current setting or historic?
3. Is there unspoken angst/frustration in any of your team dynamics currently that needs addressing?
4. Where do we need to call out/speak up for restoration of relationship in our sphere of influence?

PAUL FRIEND

We are called to be united, but we often settle for friendly. Friendly isn't united, it's keeping people happy. Unity means oneness!

Chapter 9
Fiercely United

"Believers are never told to become one; we already are one and are expected to act like it."
Joni Eareckson Tada[230]

"Behold, how good and pleasant it is when brothers dwell in unity!"
Psalm 133 v 1[231]

I once was in a gathering of youth workers where we were talking about unity and working together and what that meant for schools work. As part of this, I asked the question, "How does this work in practice? Do we advertise our own church groups when in school? Do we point to other churches' clubs?" One youth worker replied, saying that he had recommended that a young person go to another church youth group as there were more young people their age. He thought it might be a better fit for that young person. Straight away, another youth worker was so shocked he immediately jumped in and said that this youth worker should be sacked and that his job should be growing his youth, not sending them to another church.

---

[230] Joni Eareckson Tada Spontaneous Compassion, Tabletalk, November, 2008, p. 68

[231] Holy Bible, Psalm 133:1, New International Version®, NIV® Copyright ©1973, 1978, 1984, 2011 by Biblica

I stood back for a moment, shocked at the strength of the statement that this youth worker should be sacked for, in my view, having a bigger picture approach, a Kingdom approach, you could say. And, yet the statement also, in a tiny way, reflected a part of my heart that wants my own ministry to succeed and grow before anyone else's. Perhaps, when it comes to unity the biggest problem is me.

Unity is a topic that we all know is a good thing, we know it's biblical. But we all, if we are honest, like to have unity on our own terms or when it benefits us. In Philippians 2:2–5 it says:

"Therefore, if you have any encouragement from being united with Christ, if any comfort from his love, if any common sharing in the Spirit, if any tenderness and compassion, then make my joy complete by being like-minded, having the same love, being one in spirit and of one mind. Do nothing out of selfish ambition or vain conceit. Rather, in humility value others above yourselves, not looking to your own interests but each of you to the interests of the others. In your relationships with one another, have the same mindset as Christ Jesus"[232]

In verse two, Paul is appealing to us by asking if we have been in anyway encouraged by being in relationship with Jesus and received any comfort from knowing his love at all. In other words, you have had these things in abundance, so be like minded. The Greek literally means

---

[232] Holy Bible, Philippians 2:2–5, New International Version®, NIV® Copyright ©1973, 1978, 1984, 2011 by Biblica

"think the same thing."[233] Let nothing be done through selfish ambition or conceit. Selfish ambition, self-seeking and rivalry, which always lead to factions and division, must not rear its ugly head among you, Paul is saying. The only way to counter things being done through selfish ambition or conceit is through cultivating "lowliness of mind"[234] or humility. Our attitude or mindset should be as Jesus.

That all of them may be one

Jesus fiercely desired and prayed that his Church would be One. In John 17, we find his final prayer before his arrest. Jesus prays that he may be glorified, then he prays for his disciples and finally he prays for all believers to come. This is a pivotal moment. A moment when we will surely get a window into the first priority of Jesus. Surely, he will pray for the Gospel to reach every tribe and tongue, perhaps for integrity or for mass conversions and favour for his followers. But his priority and, therefore, his prayer was for unity:

"My prayer is not for them alone. I pray also for those who will believe in me through their message, that all of them may be one, Father, just as you are in me and I am in you. May they also be in us so that the world may believe that you have sent me. I have given them the glory that you gave me, that they may be one as we are one. I in them and you in me, so that they may be brought to

---

[233] Albert Barnes, Notes on the Bible, Philippians 2 v 2, 1834

[234] Holy Bible, Philippians 2:2–5, King James Version, Cambridge Edition, 1769

complete unity. Then the world will know that you sent me and have loved them even as you have loved me." John 17:20–23[235]

Jesus chooses to pray for all Christians to be one. He knew that Satan brings division and disunity and that this would be his main tactic. Spurgeon once wrote, "Satan always hates Christian fellowship; it is his policy to keep Christians apart. Anything which can divide saints from one another he delights in. He attaches far more importance to godly intercourse than we do. Since union is strength, he does his best to promote separation."[236] I wonder what Jesus thinks about all the denominations that now exist around the world. There is, of course, nothing wrong with different styles of church, in fact we need them to reach more people, but so many churches have formed out of fallouts and disunity. Perhaps knowing what lay ahead, he desired more than anything else that his bride would be united as he and the Father are united. The fact that he draws on his relationship with the Father suggests something more than just acknowledging each other's existence. This is a unity that allows for difference but is deeply formed in love and relationship. David Guzik commented on this verse saying, "Jesus prayed that they would be one and one after the pattern of the unity of God the Father and God the Son… The unity Jesus prayed for among His people has a pattern. Even as the Father and the Son are one yet are not the

---

[235] Holy Bible, John 17"20-23, New International Version®, NIV® Copyright ©1973, 1978, 1984, 2011 by Biblica

[236] https://gracequotes.org/quote/satan-always-hates-christian-fellowship-it-is-his-policy-to-keep-christians-apart-anything-which-can-divide-saints-from-one-another-he-delights-in-he-attaches-far-more-importance-to-godly-intercour/

same, we do not expect that genuine Christian unity will mean uniformity or unity of structure. It will mean unity of spirit, unity of heart, unity of purpose and unity of destiny."[237] This describes something more profound than a lot of united church services I've gone along to.

Why does Jesus' desire for us to be united so much? The answer is found in the text where he says, "So that the world may believe that you have sent me." There is a direct link to how united the Church is to people believing that Jesus is the Son of God, sent by the Father to save us. If we fall out, split, hate or ignore one another, the world watches on and sees hypocrisy and nothing more than a social club that has gone wrong.

Of course, at this birth point of the Church and throughout the epistles there was one church. In fact, throughout the next few hundred years this was the case, but we have made up for that in the last few decades! I once had a church leader say to me that they as a church could not work with us as we were a para-church organisation, that this wasn't biblical as the church should be doing what we are doing. I was a bit taken aback and thought, technically, denominations are not biblical! Don't get me wrong, denominations are helpful, having accountability structures and support is so needed and belonging to something bigger, a sense of people who share the same values, style creates a sense of a tribe. However, Jesus wasn't simply praying that we might be one with those who are like us. That isn't what he said at all. There is a call for all to be one. Hold on a minute! Does that mean we must be united with those who have

---

[237] David Guzik, Enduring Word, John 17, 2018

opposing theology and weird (to us) practices and ways of doing things? I'd suggest from this prayer the answer is yes. If it simply meant be united with those like you, then that is far more achievable. But going after unity that costs us because we don't agree or we find them difficult to relate with, that is far more challenging.

I find it interesting that in most church job descriptions, whatever the role, the place of working together with other churches tends to be the last bullet point. It is almost an acknowledgement that if you have done everything else that is our main priority then you can do some unity things—but only if you have time. Perhaps in light of Jesus' prayer, putting partnership and unity at the top would be a better aim. Let our ministry flow from this and have unity as a top priority, as it seemed to be for Jesus. One of the challenges of unity on a local level is that this is where past fallouts and hurts can still reside. There can be a sense of competition or frustration around what the big church is doing. We find it easier to relate with our tribe and so we say that that is our unity piece of work. I'm not sure, though, that this is what Jesus meant. People in your community will know that Jesus loves you and was sent from God to you if you are united, not with all the other churches in your movement, but with the churches in your village, town or city. Ruth Haley Barton writes, "Unity is not just one good priority among many. It seemed to be all Jesus wanted as everything else fell away and he faced his death. For those of us who are leaders in Christ's Kingdom, there is nothing more important than seeking this unity with all our hearts."[238]

---

[238] Ruth Haley Barton, Strengthening the Soul of your Leadership, IVP, 2018, Pg 186

This is challenging, nothing more important and with all our hearts. Is this, I wonder, true of us?

Jesus intercedes on our behalf that we may be one. He intercedes for us now and I'm sure his number one priority still is that we might be one, even amid all our different theological understandings, styles and traditions. Jesus still fiercely fights for our unity.

So what are the blockages for us when it comes to unity? What things rise up in us and hinder us from true unity?

It takes longer to do it together: If I'm honest, one of the main reasons I find unity difficult is that it takes a lot longer to do it together. I just want it done now rather than having to deal with someone else and their church's processes and decision making. I get full of impatience and want things done my way. When I was leading a local church, we used to run a village fun day as both churches as a gift to the village. To be honest, our church provided the majority of the set-up, planning and delivery and so, sometimes, people would say to me, "Can't we just do it ourselves? We are virtually doing it all anyway!" My simple response was, "No." We want the village to see that this is the churches working together demonstrating we are "one Church" in the village. Even if we do all the work and they get all the credit, I don't care as long as the village know this is the Church reaching out to them. The message was more important than the method.

They think and do things differently: I sometimes catch myself thinking, "But we can't work with them because they do things differently to us." The harsh truth is that this is simply pride. What I am really saying is that I am better than them. Don't get me wrong, sometimes we need to not partner with people if it becomes harmful or hurtful to others (more on this later). But my experience is that we are quick to say no to partnership and unity rather than to say an unreserved YES!

Unforgiveness and writing others off: We often don't do "unity" because we are harbouring unforgiveness towards others. They hurt or disappointed us before, so we won't go there again. It's a good job Jesus doesn't do that to me, but I shamefully do think like this sometimes. This is not OK. We need to move through forgiveness to a pursuing relationship and unity again. Sometimes, this unforgiveness is from before our involvement but, somehow, the bad feeling remains even though it was nothing to do with the leaders there or with you now. Sometimes, as a result of previous experience, we write others off. Maybe people didn't turn up or didn't pull their weight in terms of unity, maybe it's someone in another church or maybe a volunteer in your team of helpers and so you have written them off. They won't be involved again; we think to ourselves. Paul had a similar experience with John Mark, who he wrote off and later was reconciled to when he realised he was wrong. Who have you written off who God is asking you to show mercy to?

Low priority: Maybe we don't pursue unity because it's not a high enough priority for us. At the end of the day, it's not on my job spec and so is an optional bolt-on. Well, it is Jesus' priority; he cares passionately about our interpersonal relationships more than our activity, I'm sure and so he wants us to demonstrate the unity of the trinity expressed in how we unite with one another.

Empire v Kingdom: In a world all about improving yourself, making your mark, being successful and even on social media promoting yourself, it is so easy to be dragged into the world's way of thinking on success. We make it about the numbers and comparison with nearby churches and projects instead of simply being faithful to what God has asked us to do. Ruth Haley Barton adds, "Within my own heart was the tendency to look longingly at someone else's field and wish that mine were a little more like theirs."[239] God calls us to faithfulness not success. This is something I struggle with because I want to be successful, but I am learning that being faithful, even in the difficult decisions and walking in obedience is way more fulfilling and life-giving than disobedient success hunting, which ends up leaving us hollow. It is so easy to get caught up in seeking to build our own little empire, we all want our church, our ministry to grow and make a bigger impact but that drive for growth can become unhealthy, leading us to jealousy or competitiveness with neighbouring ministries. We have to get to a point where we accept that if the best thing for the Kingdom of God is our thing not growing, shrinking or dying, that something else might thrive in its place. As painful as that might be we will say yes to it. Choose to bless and encourage other churches and ministries, even doing this financially or with space and resources to put weight behind your words that you are genuinely about building Kingdom. Nothing shouts "Kingdom" more than one church sacrificing for the sake of another.

The truth is that we are called to be united, but we often settle for friendly. Friendly isn't united, it's keeping people

---

[239] Ruth Haley Barton, Strengthening the Soul of your Leadership, IVP, 2018

happy. Unity means oneness! That means we are supposed to be pursuing opportunities for oneness and unity. Therefore, we should also be resisting things that pull us away from one another. Resisting doing our own thing when we could do it together. The challenge in larger churches or projects is that there is so much going on that it is hard to do it together with other churches. But our absence from unity projects ends up speaking loudly about what we prioritise, even if we really don't want to be lone rangers ploughing our own furrow, that is what we communicate. We need to walk fiercely and humbly with big Kingdom hearts not allowing competitiveness to stir up within us.

So how do we practically go after unity? What does it look like for us to model in our teams a Kingdom not Empire attitude and action?

1. Make friends with those who are different from you; eat together, pray together. It's easy to stay in our own camp with those who are similar to us. You ought to seek out those who are different from you. Find those in your village, town or city who are brothers and sisters but who worship differently or think differently on issues. You don't go to convert people to your theology but to listen, to learn. Finding time to eat and pray with other church leaders or comparative ministry leaders to yourself will help break down the walls of competitiveness and scepticism and enable friendship to grow. I am humbled by the way Jesus ate and spent time with the Pharisees as well as the Samaritan woman and the tax collectors, basically any and everyone! He certainly wasn't afraid of opposing world views or

being asked questions. In fact, he loves to ask questions himself. Growing a kingdom heart that is inquisitive and humbly seeking to learn is to be fiercely humble.

2. Unite around mission not theology

It is so easy to find things to disagree on. Over the years, I've had far too many emails, phone calls or meetings with people deeply hurt and unwilling to partner or even associate with other Christians because of their views on (fill the blank). Starting from a viewpoint of friendship and prayer for each other is the best place to start. We all have differing views on a multiple range of subjects, so instead of trying to mould people into our image we need to make friends and choose to unite around mission not theology. CS Lewis wrote, "True friends face in the same direction, toward common projects, interests, goals."[240] Facing in the same direction as other churches and individuals enables unity. The common projects could be around social action projects or other outward facing initiatives. Dwight Moody commented that, "I have never yet known the Spirit of God to work where the Lord's people were divided."[241] If we are to take Jesus' prayer seriously and pursue unity fiercely, we need to unite with our family. Often uniting around mission leads to uniting around prayer or vice versa. If we build a friendship and

---

[240] https://www.goodreads.com/quotes/317586-true-friends-don-t-spend-time-gazing-into-each-other-s-eyes#:~:text=True friends don't spend time gazing into each other's,all, towards a common Lord.

[241] https://moodycenter.org/the-quotable-moody-d-l-moody-quotes/

then partner on outward facing things and pray together, we will begin to build unity that is more than tokenism. Corrie Ten Boom said, "Be united with other Christians. A wall with loose bricks is not good. The bricks must be cemented together."[242]

I am once again humbled by the fact that Jesus prays that we may be one and not just one from a distance but one just like He and the Father are one. One in relationship! This is not a fake oneness or trying to present as if we are together. This is real unity. Real unity is what Jesus yearns. He doesn't ask for unity just with those we agree with, or we consider to be theologically sound, but unity with those that believe in him. This is a high bar and one I know I fail at often, but it is what he desires for us and, therefore, if we are seeking to walk in the way of Jesus, we must step closer to those around us—even those we fundamentally disagree with.

---

[242] https://www.bc4gc.org/blog/2021/06/13/week-of-june-13

FIERCE HUMILITY

Pause | Selah

There is only one God, There is only one King; There is only one Body, That is why we sing:

Bind us together, Lord, Bind us together, With cords that cannot be broken. Bind us together, Lord, Bind us together, Bind us together with love.[243]

---

[243] Bob Gillman, Bind us Together

Questions for reflection/discussion

1. What is stopping/holding you back from throwing yourself at unity?

2. Is there some pride you need to repent of? Is there some jealousy you are holding onto?

3. Is there some unforgiveness towards another or some resentment or distrust that you need to get rid of today?

4. Who is God challenging you to work with more closely? Who is God calling you to unite with in your setting right now?

To lead is to give your time, your energy and your resources serving others and forgetting about yourself. Any other type of leadership is not leadership at all, it's leading-your-own-ship.

Chapter 10
Fiercely Serving

"People of loving service are rare in any walk of life. Leaders of loving service are still rarer. But in all cases, those who serve will be loved and remembered when those who cling to power and privileges are forgotten."
Archbishop Justin Welby[244]

"Even if I am being poured out like a drink offering on the sacrifice and service coming from your faith, I am glad and rejoice with all of you."
Philippians 2:17[245]

I'll never forget the moment I stirred from my sleep in the middle of a residential some years ago. We all slept on church floors, roll-mats and sleeping bags... the kind of night's sleep that leaves you with a bad back for months! We were part way through a three-day football camp and after a long day of coaching and tournaments, I'd got off to sleep pretty quickly. But then, in the middle of the night, I stirred as I saw the guy next to me getting back into his sleeping bag. The guy in question was called Josh and was studying with SWYM after travelling over from India. I asked Josh if all was OK. He replied that

---

[244] https://www.archbishopofcanterbury.org/speaking-writing/sermons/archbishop-canterburys-sermon-state-funeral-her-majesty-queen-elizabeth-ii

[245] Holy Bible, Philippians 2:17, New International Version®, NIV® Copyright ©1973, 1978, 1984, 2011 by Biblica

everything was fine. It was only after some probing further questions that the truth began to come out. I gradually discovered that one of the young people had woken up and had vomited. Josh had gone and comforted the young person, cleaned up all the vomit and settled the young person back to sleep before going back to bed himself. I genuinely believe that if I hadn't stirred, Josh would never have told me about it. He simply served without praise or credit; it was Christ-like serving. It is the kind of serving that prefers others, not self-promoting but looking for nothing in return. If it was me in the same situation, I'd have had to get all the leaders up, figure out a plan, work out who was doing what. Well, maybe a slight exaggeration but I'm not sure I would have been quite so silent about it as Josh was.

Jesus fiercely served. His life was an act of service to all humanity. He redefined leadership by turning upside down what the world thinks about power and authority by fiercely humbling himself to serve rather than to be served.

Jesus Served us when we were at our worst

The image of the Cross is a brutal one. The extent of the suffering in every way possible is hard to compute and understand over two thousand years later. In Gethsemane, Jesus is faced with the decision to go through with the plan, feeling the weight of what is coming on his shoulders and yet he says, "Not my will but yours be done."[246] He chooses to serve. Jesus went to the Cross and served us not because we are nice people but whilst we are at our absolute worst. "Whilst we were still sinners Christ died for us."[247] When you were at your most unlovable, most selfish, Jesus went there for you. All the sin of the world upon his shoulders, those so deformed by their sin, or the sin done unto them, those who deliberately harm others, he died for them. He died for every single murderer on the planet, every single God hater, every racist, sexist, anger-raged person. Those that spat on him, those who spit at him now. He chose to serve us when we were unfaithful, deliberately running from him, as Romans 5:6 explains, "You see just at the right time, when we were still powerless, Christ died for the ungodly."[248] While we were powerless and, in every way, ungodly, he served and died because he came to serve.

Jesus serves us now in kindness and attentive love

Jesus served us ultimately through the Cross and the resurrection, but he continues to serve us. It is easy for us to think that Jesus did his act of service and then got all the praise, adoration, honour, authority and now he's in

---

[246] Holy Bible, Luke 22:42, New International Version®, NIV® Copyright ©1973, 1978, 1984, 2011 by Biblica

[247] Holy Bible, Romans 5:8, New International Version®, NIV® Copyright ©1973, 1978, 1984, 2011 by Biblica

[248] Holy Bible, Romans 5:6, New International Version®, NIV® Copyright ©1973, 1978, 1984, 2011 by Biblica

the sweet spot up in heaven being waited on hand and foot for eternity. Now's his time to be served. But this is not our God. To serve to get something back, this is not the God I know. The incredible thing about our God is He serves and keeps on serving. Again, it's easy to think that if we serve then we'll get to one day be served and get all the top positions where we don't have to serve any longer. This is not the call of Jesus. The call of Jesus is to serve and keep on serving.

We can all think, I'm sure, about times when Jesus has served us in lots of different ways. Maybe we've been reading the Bible and, by His Spirit, God has spoken to us and taken Scripture and made it come alive to us. It feels like it was just for us—His Spirit serving us! I'm sure you have got lots of examples of little prayers offered and big answers received. The little touches of kindness, perhaps the way God uses interactions to bless us, His provision for us, the people He puts around us. Jesus has served us in the big picture of the Cross and the resurrection, but He continues to reach out and to serve us with little everyday kindnesses and on top of that he is preparing a place for us. He keeps on serving us and, right now, we are told He is interceding for us even right now as you are reading this. He prays for us, He cheers us on, he wills us on to become like Him. He fights for us; He stands in the gap with and for us all.

Not so with you

Jesus fiercely fought against pride and the desire for position and one of the best examples of this is the outrageous scene in Matthew 20, which we also find in

Mark. Now in Mark, James and John come to Jesus to make the audacious request themselves, whereas Matthew adds that they also brought their mother with them. If they did take their mother with them, it was almost certainly to aid Jesus' agreement to their request by respecting and honouring the mother. It was a sneaky move from the disciples but of course Jesus sees straight through it.

In Matthew, all three come theatrically on their knees before him. They were really trying hard; this was clearly planned out. Mark 10:35 says that they approached Jesus saying, "We want you to do for us whatever we ask."[249] This is borderline begging him now. Jesus responds, "What do you want me to do for you?"[250] I can imagine the disciples turning around and wondering what on earth these two were about to say, silence breaking out in the room as they waited for their answer. "Grant that one of these two sons of mine may sit at your right and the other at your left in your kingdom."[251] Wow! They asked, or their mum asked on their behalf, that they might have the highest places of honour, seated at his right and his left. This was a request for position, for importance, for honour, for all eternity.

---

[249] Holy Bible, Mark 10:35, New International Version®, NIV® Copyright ©1973, 1978, 1984, 2011 by Biblica

[250] Holy Bible, Mark 10:36, New International Version®, NIV® Copyright ©1973, 1978, 1984, 2011 by Biblica

[251] Holy Bible, Matthew 20:21, New International Version®, NIV® Copyright ©1973, 1978, 1984, 2011 by Biblica

Jesus' response is to ask if they can drink the cup he is about to drink, the cup of suffering and they boldly, without really knowing what they were saying, replied, "We are able."[252] So desperate for importance and being in the best position, they would do whatever it took in their minds. Jesus then explains that they will indeed drink from the cup of suffering in time but that these seats of honour they desire are not for him to grant. Then Jesus says, "These places belong to those for whom they have been prepared."[253] I don't know about you but this reply sounds a bit like what my mum used to say to me when I asked what was for pudding, she would gently say, "Wait and see." In other words, don't concern yourself with this right now. Then we hear that the ten other disciples, when they heard "became indignant with James and John".[254] At first sight, it is easy to think that this indignation was the shock of the request, a disapproving frustration with these two who had asked such a question. But we soon see that they were indignant with them because they had asked what everyone else was thinking but had said it first. How dare they? I wanted the seat of honour.

I cannot imagine how downhearted Jesus must have felt at this point. He had spent such a lot of time teaching, modelling, living a life of fierce humility in front of his

---

[252] Holy Bible, Matthew 20:22, New International Version®, NIV® Copyright ©1973, 1978, 1984, 2011 by Biblica

[253] Holy Bible, Mark 10:40, New International Version®, NIV® Copyright ©1973, 1978, 1984, 2011 by Biblica

[254] Holy Bible, Matthew 20:24, New International Version®, NIV® Copyright ©1973, 1978, 1984, 2011 by Biblica

disciples and then this! Had they not understood a thing? They were so wildly far away from the servant model of Jesus; I wonder what was going on in Jesus' mind at this moment. Whatever he was thinking he knew this was significant enough that he wanted to call a team meeting.

"Jesus called them together and said, "You know that those who are regarded as rulers of the Gentiles lord it over them and their high officials exercise authority over them. Not so with you. Instead, whoever wants to become great among you must be your servant and whoever wants to be first must be slave of all. For even the Son of Man did not come to be served, but to serve and to give his life as a ransom for many.' Mark 10:42–45[255]

Jesus took the opportunity to use the world's leadership structures—in this case the Romans and how they lorded it over and exercised authority over their subjects. It's as if Jesus is saying, "Look around you, look at your culture and how you've always seen power and authority in your society." Then the four words which, to me, model the fierceness of Jesus' pursuit of servanthood as a mark of his Kingdom: "Not so with you." You are not to lead like this. This is not how it is to be in my Kingdom, you have got it all wrong. STOP! Not so with you! Whoever wants to be great among you! Notice that Jesus isn't suggesting that ambition is a bad thing, far from it. Emma Ineson makes a good point adding, "We need to stop talking about the wrong kind of ambition and to start talking about the right kind of ambition. When motivated by a desire to serve others, to seek the kingdom and if it is

---

[255] Holy Bible, Mark 10:42–45, New International Version®, NIV® Copyright ©1973, 1978, 1984, 2011 by Biblica

undergirded by appropriate humility, ambition is not out of bounds for the Christian leader. Although our natural human inclination might be to seek after personal gain and our insecurities often lead us to seek recognition, approval and glory for the wrong reasons, ambition redeemed, matured as vocation and given over to God in the service of others and of his mission can be used by him to contribute to the growth and flourishing of the kingdom."[256]

Jesus is saying that if you want to seek after making a difference and changing the world, then you must be a servant. If you want to be first you must be a slave to all; not just a slave to the King, given over for the needs of others. Why? Because Jesus didn't come to be served, but to serve. He didn't come to get the seat of honour but to get off it. He didn't come to be lifted up; he came to lower himself. He came to give his life as a ransom for many. So, this cry "not so with you" is a command to both those twelve caught in a competitive pursuit of position and honour and success. And it is also to all who would follow them and who struggle with the same desires. Not so with you, Jesus calls to you now as you read this. Not so with you! There is a better way.

The truth is that to be a leader is to serve. To be a leader is to take responsibility and not run from it. To be quick to say sorry, as mentioned above; to be the one who takes the flack; to be kind when someone says something harsh, not to be a pushover and, therefore, sometimes lovingly pointing things out. However, most of the time it's to be gentle and kind in the face of difficulty. To lead is to

---

[256] Emma Ineson, Ambition, SPCK, 2019, Pg 43

give your time, your energy and your resources serving others and forgetting about yourself. Any other type of leadership is not leadership at all, it's leading-your-own-ship. If it's about you, you will very quickly hit the rocks as you have to face criticism, unmet expectations and you'll quit if it's not really all about serving others, as Jesus has served you.

Choosing to serve

"We need to have a servant heart!" I totally agree with this statement and yet I think in Christian circles we have got the application of this statement a bit wrong. To have a servant heart is not to have a heart transplant by the Holy Spirit. Most of the time, it comes as we serve and choose to serve when we don't want to. It's choosing to do the dirty jobs, the inconvenient jobs and to look for opportunities to serve. As we say yes and keep saying yes to serving, we, I believe, begin to develop a servant heart.

What would it look like to serve as Jesus has served you: to be willing to die for someone, to prefer them all the time; to die to your attention; your comfort; your reputation, your rights or pleasures; your dreams? To make a conscious decision to serve and keep serving? To follow in his footsteps means to serve those who in the natural world don't deserve to be served? It's to serve regardless of what people think of you, what people have said to you. It's to take joy in loving the unlovely, to take joy in releasing someone else from having to do something. It's in choosing to act, to think, to speak, to love. It's choosing to die to your right to a fair trial as

Jesus did, in choosing to die to your right to be right or be treated fairly, in choosing to die to your judgements over others and thinking that you are a better person than them. To follow in his footsteps means to look for opportunities to practice serving others in kindness and attentive love. It means to choose to go the extra mile.

To serve is to not be so wrapped up in our baggage that we miss a chance to show someone some kindness and attentive love. It's a choice but we can bless and serve others if we choose to. To wash your flatmates car when they don't ask you; to buy that chocolate bar for that volunteer which you know they'll really appreciate; to sacrifice yourself for others; to invite that person around for dinner who you don't really like that much but you know it would mean the world to. Choosing to serve in the little and the big ways takes time and energy and sacrifice. It means letting others speak when you really want to say something; it's remembering what someone said last time you were with them. It's dying to ourselves and not thinking about ourselves all the time and choosing to serve and not to be served.

I want SWYM to be known as a community of people passionate about Jesus who serve one another well. Over the years, I've been to far too many youth leader or church leader gatherings where it has felt like a competition. Who is doing well, what numbers are you seeing come to your things, baptised etc. I am so fiercely against that kind of culture that we have one of our core values as a Servant Hearted Community. This means that we seek to serve one another, to prefer one another. How I describe it is that when we come together, we know that people have our backs, so we don't have to look out for our own. Instead, we can choose to prefer, to listen well to, to honour and prefer, to celebrate and mourn with all the others in the community. I believe it is why people find the best way of describing our community is as a family. We seek to have depth of relationship, love and care that means it's more than a network, a training scheme. It's a servant-hearted community.

The truth is we can't help but be selfish, we can't help but we want to be served not to serve. We need a fresh revelation of the depth of the way Jesus has served us to inspire us to do the same. So often it's our insecurities that stop us serving, instead of throwing ourselves in to bless someone else. We question things: What if I get it wrong, am no good? They should do it instead. We hide behind ourselves. Or the opposite can be true when we think we are better than other people, we judge and say, "Someone else can do that," or "I'm not doing it, it's gross," or "I'm not going to do that because it puts me out." Our bent to self-wins, our ability to serve shrinks. It is a good job Jesus didn't say someone else can do that. No one else, in his case, could; it's also a good job Jesus didn't say, "It puts me out." He paid the ultimate price. He chose, out of love, setting his face like flint towards Jerusalem; he actively chose to do it for us. It's a good job he didn't say, "I'll do it later," or we'd be lost and hopeless without his ultimate serving of us through the cross.

Jesus made a conscious decision to be obedient to the Father and to serve and keep on serving. He is the Servant King. We, too, can't just sit back and hope God creates in us a servant heart. We must participate with Him and choose to serve, just like Josh cleaning up that vomit all those years ago. Serve and do not look for praise but take joy in serving the King who served us so well and continues to serve us even today. To serve is to live, to take is to slowly die. And it's our choice. Will we walk in the way of Jesus? Will it be said of us, they came to serve not to be served?

Living a life of servanthood

Often, as leaders, I think we can get sucked into a mindset of serving when I do things for God, then I have the rest of my time to do what I want with. This is not the way of Jesus.

Jesus didn't just serve when the crowds were around him. It wasn't a part-time hobby to serve, it was who he was. I once heard someone say that you know if you are a servant not when you choose to serve but when someone orders you to serve. It is in these moments we see our true heart: how we feel about being ordered around like a slave, having to do something we haven't signed up for. If we are to truly be a servant and a slave to all then we must be prepared to serve and keep serving wherever we are. What does this look like, practically?

To live a life of servanthood means that it starts at home with whoever you live with. Do you seek to serve them and prefer them? Often, our families, flatmates, etc., get the dregs of our energy at the end of a long day, when all we want to do is sit on the sofa. To be a servant leader begins at home. Would those in your household describe you as a servant? How do you serve your neighbours—are you a blessing to them? Will you go out of your way to help and serve them? So often, we make leadership all about the high moments, but servanthood is formed when we serve those in our everyday interactions.

As a family we have taken on an Airbnb project, which is a static caravan that we rent out at our home. I now spend a huge amount of time each summer changing bedding in the caravan. It's made me realise what a blessing it is when you stay somewhere and people strip the bed when they leave. It is so helpful. Now whenever I stay somewhere I make sure I strip the bed whether at a friend's, a Premier Inn or wherever. I usually will have a little Holy Spirit nudge on these occasions. I might think, "Well they are paid to do it." But I know the conviction of the Spirit saying, "Serve them, bless them." It is in these little inconveniences, these little choices that we begin to develop a heart to serve.

I've decided over the last few years to try to make sure that I go to serve at an event or project once a year where there is no benefit to me or my ministry. I am simply going to be a blessing and encouragement. I do this because I can get caught up in the mindset of being here to serve but knowing I am getting something out of it. There is some win for me in this action. It's good to be reminded that true service is all about the other.

Living a life of service, making the little choices enables us to lead as servants. To not serve for position or importance but to serve Christ and find joy in this alone. I am currently writing this at the end of a sabbatical which has been such a gift. As I was walking the dog this morning, I reached a point where I just poured my heart out to God saying, "I just want to be background now, to live humbly, I don't want the stage, the significance, I just want to serve humbly and be close to you." I trust I am able, with the Holy Spirit's help, to live out this prayer and not to be enticed by the lure of perceived success, importance or the crowd. Justin Welby, in his sermon at the funeral of Queen Elizabeth II, said, "The pattern for many leaders is to be exalted in life and forgotten after death. The pattern for all who serve God—famous or obscure, respected or ignored—is that death is the door to glory."[257] Life is an opportunity to serve, our treasure is not and should not be found here.

So how do we engender a fierce serving within our teams? How do we best serve those we lead in a way that shows a different way to live than lording it over them?

1. Serve your team in prayer and in practical ways

To walk in the way of Jesus means to stand in the gap for others, to serve them by praying. Practically, it's setting aside some time each day to pray for those God has given me to serve. Serving them in prayer will fuel serving them in practical action. I have a prayer book which I use to aid me in my prayers, sometimes it just lists names, other times prayers, but I enjoy spending time with God with a list of people and going on a prayer adventure with God exploring how I can encourage and serve these people today. It's prayer that fuels and motivates practical service.

---

[257] J https://www.archbishopofcanterbury.org/speaking-writing/sermons/archbishop-canterburys-sermon-state-funeral-her-majesty-queen-elizabeth-ii

It is important to make sure when around your team that you look for ways to serve them. It could be making them a drink as well as making sure you give time to find out how their week has been and listening to them attentively. A key, as a leader, is to not think anything is below us. If someone asks for help, go out of your way to help and serve. If you model acts of service and a heart that is ready to serve, then you will find your team follow in your footsteps.

2. Give others opportunities to serve in the big and the little

Within your church or organisation, make sure you are creating ways that people might be able to serve and prefer others. Sometimes, people might not see spaces to serve so sharing opportunities of how people can serve but then sometimes asking people, "Could someone...?" If we don't give or find opportunities for others to serve there is a danger people will become consumers and not give and serve. There is also a danger that we do all the serving and don't give space for others to do anything. Sometimes to serve is to step back and allow others to serve.

Pause | Selah

So let us learn how to serve, And in our lives enthrone Him, Each other's needs to prefer, For it is Christ we're serving

This is our God, The Servant King, He calls us now to follow Him, To bring our lives as a daily offering, Of worship to The Servant King

The Servant King by Graham Kendrick[258]

---

[258] Graham Kendrick, The Servant King, 1989

Questions for reflection/discussion

1. Are you living a life of service? What does serving those you live with and around look like for you practically?
2. What does a servant-hearted team look like to you?
3. How can you encourage, foster and model servanthood in your setting?
4. Who do you struggle to serve? How might you choose practically to serve these people today?

PAUL FRIEND

Conclusion

Humility, as I hope we have discovered through the pages of this book, is not an optional extra as a leader but is right at the heart of what it means to lead like Jesus. In a world which desperately seeks fame and the limelight, to lead in a different way is both countercultural and therefore very hard to do.

Humility is something to ask God to give you but is, even more so, something you must learn to walk in. Fierce humility is the kind of leadership that protects, guards and inspires those on our teams to walk the same path even when it feels like the hardest road to walk.

We must first learn to walk humbly before our God as Micah encouraged us to do[259], but then we must walk humbly before others. These two tasks will be contested daily as pride rears its ugly head, but a life of daily surrender and worship with a lot of repentance is the path we must follow. Ultimately, as RT Kendell put it so well: "Being proud of your humility, however, is an impossibility, because once you think you are humble, you just lost it." [260]

---

[259] Holy Bible, Micah 6:8, New International Version®, NIV® Copyright ©1973, 1978, 1984, 2011 by Biblica

[260] R.T Kendall, The Power of Humility, Charisma House, 2011, Pg 53

PAUL FRIEND

About the Author

Paul is married to Jo. They have two boys. Paul has been involved in Christian leadership for the last twenty-five years including leading SWYM and a local church just outside Exeter, in Devon. Paul has an MA in missional leadership and speaks regularly at conferences and churches around the Southwest as well as lecturing on a BA programme with Moorlands College. In his spare time, Paul loves spending time with family and friends, supporting Liverpool FC, any sport with a ball and a good curry and a film.

PAUL FRIEND

About the Organisation

SWYM (South West Youth Ministries) was launched in 1997 and our vision is that "Every child and young person in the South-west would encounter Jesus, come to know Him and make a choice to live for more." As we work and pray towards this vision, our main strategy is to place trainee children and youth workers with churches, local ministries and school work projects throughout the region. We also resource local churches with training events, residentials and leadership development opportunities for young people. For more information, visit www.swym.org.uk

PAUL FRIEND

About PublishU

PublishU is transforming the world of publishing.

PublishU has developed a new and unique approach to publishing books, offering a three-step guided journey to becoming a globally published author!

We enable hundreds of people a year to write their book within 100-days, publish their book in 100-days and launch their book over 100-days to impact tens of thousands of people worldwide.

The journey is transformative, one author said,

"I never thought I would be able to write a book, let alone in 100 days... now I'm asking myself what else have I told myself that can't be done that actually can?'"

To find out more visit
www.PublishU.com

PAUL FRIEND

Printed in Great Britain
by Amazon